In his delightful new book, Buchwald demolishes Republicans and Democrats with equal zeal, and takes a cold, hard look at such crucial domestic issues as sex on campus, the art of leg-watching, and is there a real J. Edgar Hoover. . . . "Buchwald's lawn is littered with the remains of sacred cows. . . . In this collection nothing—statesmen and status-seekers, marriage and parenthood, and the Beatles —is safe from the sanity of his laughter."

—Virginia Kirkus

"There are those who nostalgically yearn for Will Rogers. But Art Buchwald is, in a more sophisticated way, every bit as humorous and every bit as wise."

—Los Angeles Times

...And Then

illustrated by Laszlo Matulay

I Told
the President

the secret papers of
ART BUCHWALD

A FAWCETT CREST BOOK
Fawcett Publications, Inc., Greenwich, Conn.
Member of American Book Publishers Council, Inc.

A Fawcett Crest Book reprinted by arrangement with
G. P. Putnam's Sons. This book contains the complete
text of the original hardcover edition.

Library of Congress Catalog Card Number: 65-13289

PRINTING HISTORY
G. P. Putnam's Sons edition published April 30, 1965
First printing, March 1965
Second printing, May 1965
Third printing, June 1965

First Fawcett Crest printing, May 1966

Published by Fawcett World Library,
67 West 44th Street, New York, N. Y. 10036.
PRINTED IN THE UNITED STATES OF AMERICA.

CONTENTS

c. *The Voter*

II. ON THE BRINK OF PEACE

III. F.I.N.K.

IV. FATHERS FOR MORAL AMERICA

V. BLUE EYES AND GREEN TEETH

VI. THE NERVOUS CANARY

VII. STATUS SYMBOLS

VIII. THAT'S SHOW BIZ

IX. MAN IN A TRENCHCOAT

X. MY WAR ON POVERTY

XI. HOW ARE THINGS IN NONAMURA?

BY WAY OF AN INTRODUCTION

It was many years ago, more years than I want to remember, when I was about eleven years old and I was sitting on the river bank with my closest friend, Lyndon, fishing.

"Lyndon," I said, "what do you want to be when you grow up?"

Lyndon blushed. "You'd make fun of me if I told you."

"No, I wouldn't, honest."

"Well, I know it sounds kind of crazy, but I'd like to be President of the United States."

"Heck," I said, "every boy wants to be that. I mean what do you *really* want to be?"

"Like I told you, President of the United States."

"Now, how is a boy with your accent ever going to become President?"

"I haven't figured it out yet, but I know this. I love all the people and want to be their leader."

"Lyndon," I said, "I want to talk some sense into you. I know this place ain't much around here, but you work it. Maybe you'll never be rich, and maybe you'll never be famous, but at least you'll have something to call your own."

"Arty Bird," Lyndon said, "I love this place. I love the cactus and I love the soil. I love the trees and the hills. I love the sun coming up in the morning and going down at night. I love fishing in the river and hunting in the hills. But if I have to live somewhere, I'd rather live in Washington."

I studied my friend and saw a far-off look in his eye.

"Well, let's, for argument's sake, say you were President of the United States. What would you do?" I asked him.

"First, I'd wage a war on poverty. Then I'd ask for medical care for old people. Then I'd ask for money to educate our children, kids like you and me who could easily be dropouts. Then I'd build a new canal to replace the one in Panama."

"What for?"

11

"We can always use another canal."

"Where you going to get all the money for this?"

"I'd make some economies in our spending. For one thing, I'd turn out all the lights in the White House. Then I'd close the Brooklyn Navy Yard, and finally I'd do away with the Army Reserve."

"Lyndon, you're sure talking crazy."

"I know it's a dream, but I have to start somewhere."

"You think you're going to get Congress to let you do all those things?"

"If they don't," Lyndon said, "I'll break their arms."

Lyndon pulled in a catfish.

"I must say, Lyndon, when you dream, you sure dream big," I said.

Lyndon put another worm on his hook. "You know something else? When I get elected, it's going to be by the largest number of votes any President ever got."

I rolled on the grass, laughing with glee. "You're really something, Lyndon!"

"You can laugh all you want to. But I'm willing to take you with me the whole way."

"No, thank you," I said. "I got plans of my own."

It's lucky I didn't take him up on his offer, because I heard years later that my boyhood friend and fishing partner, whose name was Lyndon Schwartz, gave up his dreams of becoming President, and went into the pants business with his father.

I. POLITICS

a. *The President*
☆☆☆☆☆☆☆☆☆☆☆☆☆☆☆☆☆☆☆

THAT'S FRIENDSHIP

When Barry Goldwater spoke in Greensburg, Pennsylvania, he said, "I have served in the United States Senate for the last twelve years and I have had some of the most hair-pulling debates I ever want to have with Hubert Humphrey, but I don't think two people in this country are closer together as friends. And with Lyndon Johnson I have argued, fought, and debated on the floor, in his office and my office, but we can still call each other friends. It is only when we allow disagreement to overrun and overrule good judgment that we forget our basic goodness and decency in this country."

This statement came as a surprise to many people who said this was one of the roughest, dirtiest campaigns in American history. If we were to believe Mr. Goldwater, this is what could probably have happened a few weeks after the election.

Senator Goldwater enters President Johnson's White House office. The men throw their arms around each other.

"Gosh, it's good to see you, Lyndon. It's been a long time."

"Damn right, it has, Barry, and we can't let this happen again."

Mr. Goldwater sits down. "Well, how's the old faker and phony?"

President Johnson chortles, "That was a bit rough, you trigger-happy maverick."

Mr. Goldwater slaps his sides. "You sure got mileage out of that one. I swear everyone in the country thought I was going to push the button as soon as I got in."

"I can't say you helped me much when you said I was soft on Communism," Mr. Johnson says, wagging his finger.

13

"Heck, Lyndon, I figured I'd run it up the flagpole and see who saluted. And by the way, what was all this stuff during the campaign about me being against Social Security?"

Mr. Johnson roars with laughter. "I knew that would get under your skin. You never did have much sense about the old folks' vote."

Mr. Goldwater says, "Well, you might have thought that was funny, but I didn't see you laughing when I brought up Bobby Baker, Billie Sol Estes, and Matt McCloskey."

"Heck, Barry, you didn't have any choice. I never minded that stuff at all. But I had to pretend I was upset."

Barry breaks into guffaws. "Lyndon, you are a sneaky one. You and that curious crew you got around you."

"Oh, yeah, I wanted to mention that. What was all that hogwash you were talking about concerning moral decay in America?"

"I thought I'd give you a little scare, Lyndon. I had the country thinking there for a while that we were going to hell in a basket."

Mr. Johnson hands Mr. Goldwater a bourbon. "It sure was fun."

Mr. Goldwater sips his drink and looks at his friend warmly. "I'm going to miss it, Lyndon."

The President replies, "So am I, Barry. We've had a lot of laughs these last eight weeks."

Mr. Goldwater replies, "I guess I don't know when I've enjoyed myself more."

As they're talking, Hubert Humphrey walks into the office. He sees Mr. Goldwater and rushes over to him, pumping his hand.

Mr. Goldwater grins and says, "Horatio, you no-good radical Socialist ADA dupe, how's your wife?"

"Just great, you right-wing extremist son of a John Bircher. How's Peggy?"

"She's fine. Gosh, it's wonderful for the three of us to be together again."

Both Lyndon and Hubert look at their friend fondly and raise their glasses. "Here's to you, Barry," Mr. Johnson says. "They don't make many like you anymore."

VISIT TO THE RANCH

It is not generally known that President de Gaulle planned to visit President Johnson right after the elections, but somehow plans went askew.

This is what happened.

A few days after the election President de Gaulle's Foreign Minister came into his office and said, *"Monsieur le président,* I have just received word from our ambassador concerning your state visit to the United States. I have the tentative schedule with me."

"Good. What time do I get to Washington?"

"You're not going to Washington. You're going to the LBJ ranch in Texas."

"Alors?"

"We will fly directly from Paris to Texas, where you and Mrs. de Gaulle will be met by President Johnson and Mrs. Johnson in a golf cart."

"What is a golf cart?"

"It's a small car that Americans use to play golf in."

"Have you been drinking?"

"No, *Monsieur le président.* It is traditional on the LBJ ranch to ride around in a golf cart, and our security people feel it's safer than if you drove around with him in his Lincoln Continental."

The Foreign Minister continued. "The first thing will be a tour of the ranch. The American President will in all probability start chasing his cattle in the golf cart."

De Gaulle said, "I am not going."

"Please, Monsieur le président, listen to the rest of the schedule. After the tour you will go to the main house to rest and meet the President's relatives. Then you will be measured for a 10-gallon hat and cowboy boots."

"I have the bomb. I do not have to go."

"But, *Monsieur le président,* Chancellor Erhard did it. After the measurements, you and Mrs. de Gaulle will be escorted outside to a barbecue."

"What is a barbecue?"

"It is a Western-type dinner consisting of pork ribs, sausages, beef briskets, and chicken legs cooked over a smoky fire and smeared with a very hot sauce. It is served with hot chili beans and sourdough biscuits. For dessert there is fried apple pie, served with six-shooter coffee."

"I am not only not going, I am getting out of NATO."

"Monsieur le président, our ambassador says it is important that you and the President sit down and talk."

"When do we do that?"

"Probably after you write your names in a cement block in front of the ranch house."

"What is that?"

"You have to get on your knees and write your name in a block of cement. It takes the place of laying a wreath."

"Monsieur le ministre, I think I must ask you to resign."

"I am only repeating what is in the cable."

"But when do I get to talk to the President?" de Gaulle said.

"Right after the sheepdog act. You will witness trained dogs rounding up sheep on the ranch. It's quite moving. Then you will have your talk. After the talk there will be a joint press conference held on a bale of hay and protocol hopes you will wear your Texas hat when you appear for it."

"Is that all?" de Gaulle said.

"There is one more paragraph. The ambassador wants to know what are your feelings about getting on a horse?"

WASHINGTON ECONOMY WAVE

The big word in Washington this year is "economy." In order to impress Congress and the American people, as well as take one of the main issues away from the Republicans, President Johnson has ordered everybody in the Federal government to make every possible cut in expenditures. No one has been exempted from the economy wave, and now that the ball has started rolling it may be very hard to stop.

It could even reach the confines of the White House itself.

I hate to project what might happen, but I will. It's 1966 and the President has just been informed that his thrift program has saved the government $2 billion. He is very pleased and he says to his Administrative Assistant:

"Get me Secretary McNamara on the phone."

"Yes, sir. Do you have a dime?"

"What for?" the President wants to know.

"As an economy measure we've installed pay telephones in

your office. We felt it would make everybody realize you meant business."

President Johnson grumbles and hands his assistant a dime.

"Bob, this is the President. I was wondering if you could come over and see me right away. It's very important. What's that? You'll be over in an hour? Can't you get over any sooner? You have to take two buses from the Pentagon. I know we took your car away from you, Bob. Now calm down. Why don't you take a taxi? I'll okay it with Doug Dillon. Don't worry, Bob, you won't get in any trouble. I'll explain to him it had to do with the Berlin crisis."

The President hangs up and turns to McGeorge Bundy.

"Any word from the Kremlin in answer to my telegram concerning Laos?"

"No, sir."

"That's the third telegram they haven't answered. What do you make of it?"

"Well, sir, I think one of the problems is that we keep sending the telegrams collect."

"The Laos problem is as much their problem as mine," the President says. "If they're sincere about a settlement in Laos, they should pay for the telegrams."

As they are talking, Mrs. Johnson storms in. "I just heard you're having a state dinner for General de Gaulle and 600 people tonight."

"Yes, dear."

"Did you know the cook has been laid off? And all the footmen?"

The President looks at his assistant, who says, "It's all taken care of, sir. We're sending out to a Chinese restaurant for 600 meals. The Comptroller says we can save $650 without a White House cook."

"But who is going to serve the food?" Mrs. Johnson demands.

"It comes in individual cartons, Mrs. Johnson," the assistant says. "And there won't be any dishes to wash once the dinner is over."

Mrs. Johnson slams the door.

The President says, "Get me Jack Valenti."

"He's cutting the White House lawn, sir. And I must say he's doing as good a job as the gardener. It's been quite a saving."

"Is everything ready for my trip to the ranch?"

"Yes, sir. There was only one question. Did you want to fly American Airlines or TWA?"

"You mean my plane—"

"Yes, sir. It was sold to General Motors."

The President takes a dime out of his pocket and calls Horace Busby. "Horace, I'd like you to whip up a new speech for me. Something along the lines of we've got to spend money in order to make money. And don't mention anything about economy, please. I know you don't have a typewriter. Write it in longhand and I'll have it typed over here."

SHE COULD HAVE DANCED ALL NIGHT

There are two definite status symbols attached to the Johnson Administration. One is swimming with the President in your birthday suit in the White House pool, if you're a man, and the other is dancing with him, if you're a woman, at a White House reception. If our present-day historians are correct, there is nothing the President likes to do more than to swim and dance, and he doesn't like to do either alone.

In the past I have been treated to first-person accounts of how it is to dance with the President of the United States. There is hardly a female reporter in Washington who hasn't danced with President Johnson, and if the President is having trouble finding 50 women for high places in government, he is having no trouble finding 50 women to foxtrot with.

Therefore I was as surprised as anyone to find a young lady from one of the leading American newspapers sobbing uncontrollably at the west gate of the White House one morning.

I held her in my arms until she calmed down and then asked her what the trouble was.

"I'm a wallflower at the White House," she said.

"That's not true," I said. "Everyone likes you."

"No, no, no," she sobbed. "It is true. I've been to two dinners and three receptions and the President hasn't asked me to dance once."

"You mustn't take it personally," I told her. "The President can't dance with everyone."

"Yes, he can," she said, "and he has. That's why I'm so unhappy."

"Well," I said, trying to cheer her up, "when you get right down to it, it isn't very important, is it?"

"That's what you think. I've gotten an exclusive interview with Bobby Baker, I broke the story on Panama, I was the first one who wrote about the water being shut off at Guantanamo Bay, and all my editor keeps asking me is, 'When are you going to dance with President Johnson?' "

"You are in trouble. Tell me, have you consulted Arthur Murray?"

"Yes. I signed up for a lifetime course, but he said all he could do was to teach me how to dance. He couldn't guarantee that the President would dance with me."

"Well, at least he's honest," I said. "Couldn't you pretend you'd danced with President Johnson?"

She shook her head. "The other female reporters keep track. I know one reporter whom he's danced with twice, and she has half the circulation my paper does."

"Then he doesn't select his partners according to circulation?"

"It doesn't look that way. It's done on pure favoritism."

"Perhaps *you* could ask the President to dance?" I suggeste .

"The Secret Service won't let me," she said, starting to bawl again.

Just then a White House policeman came up and said, "All right, move along. No crying in front of the White House."

"You don't understand, officer. This poor lady is crying because President Johnson hasn't danced with her."

"That's funny," he said with surprise. "He danced with my wife just the other night."

THE PRESIDENT'S NEWS CONFERENCE

President Johnson's news conference of March, 1964, was considered one of his best. Instead of going on at 11 o'clock on Saturday morning, as he did the previous week, he selected the prime time of 3:30 in the afternoon, which should have given him a TV rating of .3, or one out of every 800,000 homes in the country.

To make sure the President wouldn't have too large an audience, the conference wasn't announced until noon of the same Saturday. And then to make sure that not everyone who tuned him in would listen to the news conference, the President spent the first nine minutes announcing appointments he had made, quoting from Dow-Jones averages, statistics of the National Association of Purchasing Agents and the cost-of-living index for January.

But you can't keep this kind of exciting news forever, and the fear in Washington is that the President, if he continues his Saturday news conferences, will soon run out of hard news.

I hate to imagine what will happen 20 Saturdays from now if the President keeps up this pace.

"Good afternoon, ladies and gentlemen. I have a few announcements to make. My daughter Luci passed her algebra examination and Lynda Bird has been invited to a dance next week in Annapolis. I wish to announce several important appointments. I am appointing John L. McQuade as night porter at the Sitting Bull, Wyoming, Courthouse for a four-year term. I am reappointing George Martin as a guard at Leavenworth Federal Prison, and Harold Richmond has agreed to continue to serve in his capacity as attendant at the Veterans Hospital in Denver.

"My search for qualified women in government continues. I am happy to announce that Mrs. Gisella Meally has agreed to become an upstairs maid at the White House, and I have appointed Mrs. Carlton Peabody as assistant cook at Blair House. Miss Harriet Clingpeaches has agreed to serve as a baby-sitter at Oak Ridge, Tennessee. Mrs. P. K. Wratingbottom, a prominent Kansas City matron, has been appointed chairman of the car pool at Thomas Jefferson High School.

"New den mothers for the Cub Scouts in Washington, D. C., are as follows: Mrs. Samuel Lanahan, Mrs. John Lindsay, Mrs. Benjamin Bradlee, Mrs. Edward Streator, and Mrs. Carleton Kent.

"I have set up several new Presidential committees. My first committee will make a study of my war-on-electricity program. The committee will advise me on how we can eliminate electric light bulbs in the United States without hurting the economy. I have also appointed a committee to make a survey of cocktail parties as they affect our unemployment situation.

"I have one more announcement. I am happy to report that I am closing down the Post Office Department, which will save the American taxpayer $235 million.

"I would like to read the census figures for 1964 state by state. If we have any time after that, I would be glad to answer any questions."

BIG BROTHER IS EVERYWHERE

I went to the gym for a little game of handball one day. As I opened one of the lockers to put my clothes in, I found one of the better-known White House correspondents inside.

"What are you doing in here?" I asked.

"Sh! Shhh!" he said. "I'm hiding from the President."

"President Johnson?"

He opened his eyes with fright. "Not so loud. He may hear you."

It was obvious that the fellow was pretty shaken up, so I helped him out of the locker and placed him on a bench.

"Now tell me what it's all about," I said soothingly.

"Well, with most Presidents I've covered it's always been a question of trying to see them. But in President Johnson's case, it's a question of trying to avoid him. Like Big Brother, he's everywhere. He never takes any time off and you never know when he's going out, whom he's going to visit, or what he's going to say. He calls press conferences at the damnedest times and he shows up at parties at the last minute, and—" The correspondent started to break down.

"Now, now," I said, "it isn't that bad."

"He never sleeps," the White House correspondent sobbed. "I haven't been home in three weeks."

"But I should think it would be a lot of fun."

"It was at the beginning," he said. "We all said, 'Boy, this is exciting.' But after a while it got to be exhausting. It's the uncertainty of it all that gets you down. You don't know where he's going next. One day he lunches with a woman correspondent at her house, the next day he shows up at a cocktail party for an aide, the next day he turns up at the Smithsonian Institution.

"And through it all he keeps calling us into his office to tell us what a great job we're doing."

"I think President Johnson is genuinely fond of the press," I said, "and he does the things he does to help you in your work. After all, he's giving you a lot to write about."

"I know I should be grateful," he said. "But how much can anybody write? Why doesn't he go to Camp David with his wife or take a boat ride on the Presidential yacht? Why doesn't he ban us from the LBJ Ranch or keep us out of the White House? We're human, too."

"That's no way to be. After all, if the President of the United States makes himself available to the press, you shouldn't complain."

"Don't get me wrong," the White House correspondent said. "I enjoy seeing the President just as much as anybody, but if I could only get a couple of days off."

"Is that why you were hiding in the locker?" I asked.

"Yes. I figured he'd never find me here. After all, he has his own swimming pool, so I thought the gym would be safe. It would have been, too, if you hadn't opened the locker."

"Why don't you take a trip somewhere?" I suggested.

"Where? He's just announced he wants to speak around the country on weekends. There's no place safe," he cried.

"Why don't you ask for another assignment?"

"I can't," he said. "He called my editor the other day and said I was doing a wonderful job. My editor says I have to stay."

"You do have a problem," I admitted. "Would you like me to put you back in the locker?"

"No"—he shrugged—"I'll go back. It's Saturday and nobody's working and it's beautiful out, so he'll probably call a press conference."

He got up to leave. "Thanks for talking to me. If he comes in here looking for me, tell him I decided to go back to the White House of my own free will."

WHERE THE PEDERNALES FLOWS

As soon as the President finished his State of the Union speech, I was ordered to get some public reaction. So I immediately called my father in Forest Hills, New York, and asked him what he thought of all the things President Johnson wanted to do.

"If he's got the money," my father said, "let him go ahead."

"I don't think he has the money, Pop."

"I knew there was a catch to it."

"What part of the speech did you like the most?"

"I liked the part when he described the land around the Pedernales River, where he lived. He said it was once covered with scrub cedar and terrible soil and the river flooded all the time. Then men worked it, and now the land is abundant with fruit, cattle, goats, and sheep, and pleasant homes and lakes. That must have been a very good real estate investment."

"That wasn't the point the President was trying to make."

"Never mind his point. I should have bought 100 acres. I'd be a rich man today."

"Pop, what the President was trying to say was men made the land what it is today."

"Of course. You don't hear of these real estate deals until it's too late. I'll bet on the basis of the President's speech land values around the Pedernales River have doubled."

"The President was talking about a dream."

"I'm talking about a dream, too," Pop said. "Suppose you subdivided the acreage and got a guy like Zeckendorf in as a partner. You know what you could make in capital gains alone?"

"Pop, you're all confused about The Great Society."

"Listen. Give me 100 acres next to Johnson's ranch and I'll do without Medicare."

"Isn't there anything else you got out of the speech?"

"Even if we didn't subdivide, the agricultural subsidies would be worth the investment. You know how much the government is paying these days for *not* raising wheat?"

"That's not the point."

"And there could be oil on the property. In Texas anything is possible. I'm glad he didn't say anything in his speech about oil depletion allowances."

"Pop, forget the land a minute. Was there any part of the President's speech you objected to?"

"I didn't care too much for the President inviting the Soviet leaders to speak to the American people on television. Suppose the Russians take up the President's invitation. Do you know what the record is for the shortest speech a Soviet leader ever delivered? Four hours and 23 minutes. I'm not sure the Americans are up to it. A wasteland we've got on television now, but Johnson's talking about Siberia."

"You may have a point there. Perhaps the President was hoping his speech would be telecast on Soviet television."

"I wouldn't like that."

"Why not?"

"You might have the Russians buying up a lot of land around the Pedernales River. Real estate values could go down."

"I can see the President's speech made a deep impression on you, Pop."

"When a man of his importance speaks, I listen. You know,

an idea just occurred to me. Why couldn't somebody develop a place down there and call it 'Barbecueland'? You don't have Walt Disney's private number, by any chance, do you?"

DISNEYLAND EAST

As every one knows, President Johnson turned the White House into "Disneyland East" last May for the benefit of Washington reporters. In one of the most blatant attempts to seduce the members of the Fourth Estate, the President told reporters he would love to have their wives and children attend his televised press conference. The newspapermen, suspicious of the invitation, vowed they would not be taken in by such an obvious ploy to win them over, and I'm happy to report that only 1,196 out of 1,200 accredited correspondents brought their families to the White House. It shows there is still integrity in the journalistic profession, no matter what the critics say.

Although I didn't bring my wife or children to the party, my reasons for doing so had nothing to do with integrity. I felt that, if he had us to his house, then we would have to have his family to ours, and my wife said she just couldn't afford to feed so many Secret Service men.

But I did go to the White House alone to see the show, and I must say it was a moving experience. The kids were moving during the entire press conference.

The thing to do if you were covering this press conference was to sit next to a youngster and get his cute impressions of the affair. Many reporter-fathers interviewed their own children, others had their children write their stories, and still others made up quotes of things their children might have said.

Since I didn't have a child of my own, I sat next to a cute little fellow with a crew cut, a tiny bow tie, and candy-striped linen sports jacket.

"What do you think of the press conference?" I asked him.

"I think it's a good idea," he replied. "It gives Johnson a change of pace and I guess he figures he can make up for all the bad beagle publicity."

"Is there anything particular that impresses you?"

"I'm surprised he's using a Teleprompter," the little fellow said. "But I imagine it's better than reading from a script."

The President started to speak. He announced he was sending Secretary McNamara to Vietnam after a visit to Bonn.

"I'm inclined to think that's a mistake," my little friend said. "He shouldn't use McNamara as an errand boy. It will make the Vietnamese lose faith in Lodge."

The President then went on to announce that he was appointing a Maritime Advisory Committee to make a study of our shipping problems.

"That's very constructive," the little fellow commented. "We've been ignoring this problem much too long, and it should have been done years ago."

The President then announced that there was an increase in the Gross National Product and that the rate of return of stockholder's equity and manufacturing corporations was 10.1 percent for 1963 and 11.4 for the last quarter of the year.

"That surprises me," the little guy said. "I thought I had read it was 11.2, but it's still impressive."

I was starting to get nervous.

When the President announced that the total working time lost to strikes in 1963 was .13 of one percent, the lowest since World War II, my friend nodded. "A very encouraging figure. It should be good for votes."

The President continued by going into detail on his Latin-American aid program. He said he planned to sign several new loan agreements and commitment letters for new South American development projects.

My little friend sighed. "Now he's lost me. I must say you have to listen to an awful lot of bilge before you can get your picture taken with the President these days."

HE'S GOT THE TOURIST VOTE

In July, 1964, it was too early to count votes, but if things continued the way they had been, President Johnson was going to wind up with the tourist vote. Probably no President had been so close to the tourist as Mr. Johnson, and vice versa.

Usually the President just shakes hands with the tourists through the fence, but one Sunday last summer President Johnson invited them into the garden for a stroll and one of the guides who sells tours around the White House promised me that the following Sunday the President was going to have everyone in for dinner.

This didn't hurt business in the least for Washington tour companies. I heard one salesman making a pitch to a group of tourists on Pennsylvania Avenue and he said, "Our tour includes a visit to the Senate, the House of Representatives, the Lincoln Memorial, the Smithsonian Institution and Mount Vernon. We then wind up at the White House, where you each will be personally met by the President of the United States."

"Will Mrs. Johnson be with him?" a lady wanted to know.

"She usually is," the salesman said, waving the tickets.

"What about Lynda Bird?" a teen-ager wanted to know.

"If Lynda Bird is in town she'll be there," he promised.

"Can I get my picture with Him and Her?" another tourist wanted to know.

"Of course. What kind of Washington tour do you think we're running?"

"How do we know when the President is coming out?" a skeptical man from Kansas asked.

"We send in word with the Secret Service," the guide assured him.

"What do you say?"

"We just say there's a bunch of tourists outside that want to meet the President and, sure enough, he comes out. The Secret Service is very cooperative and there is nothing that makes them happier than seeing the President walk around meeting 300 people he doesn't know."

"Why can't we meet him in his office?" someone asked.

"We're working on that now," the guide said. "There's talk of extending the White House tour from the public rooms to the President's office, but a few of his staff are still against it. American Express is thinking of opening a branch at the White House and if they do perhaps something could be worked out."

A little boy wanted to know if he could go swimming in the White House pool.

"We've been trying to work out swimming privileges with the President. He could use the pool from two to three and then tourists could use it from three to five, but as of now we can't guarantee you a swim as part of the tour."

"How much is the tour?"

"It's $4.90, which includes all the places mentioned as well as having your picture taken with the President."

"Suppose I don't want to meet the President? How much is the tour then?"

"I'm sorry, sir. Meeting the President is included in the package and we can't make any changes for individuals who refuse to go along with the group."

b. The Campaign
☆☆☆☆☆☆☆☆☆☆☆☆☆☆☆☆☆☆☆

HIGH NOON

We've decided to remake the very successful movie, *High Noon*. To bring it up to date, we're going to have to change the story around a bit. In our film they're having an election for sheriff, in the town of Little Elephant Horn. Much to everyone's surprise, the Arizona Kid announces he's going to run for the office. The Arizona Kid is noted for being quick on the draw and shooting first and asking questions afterward. The respectable citizens in the town are horrified at the thought of his being sheriff.

As our story opens, several of the Arizona Kid's henchmen are waiting at the station for him to arrive on the noon train.

It's 10:45 A.M. by the station clock. A small group of responsible citizens go over to visit the Old Sheriff at his farm to persuade him to come out against the Arizona Kid.

The Old Sheriff shakes his head. "Boys, I'd like to help you, but I'm getting on in years, and I don't feel it's my place to interfere. I don't like the Arizona Kid any more than you do, but I'm not going to get messed up in town politics."

"But every one respects you," the citizens plead. "If you say the Kid's irresponsible, a lot of folks are going to listen."

"Boys, you know I don't like to deal in personalities. I got my farm and my cattle and I've been through the war. I just want to settle down and be left alone."

The clock at the railroad station shows eleven o'clock and Arizona Kid's henchmen are whooping it up.

The citizens decide to ride over and see Pennsylvania Bill and ask him if he'll run against the Arizona Kid.

Pennsylvania Bill says, "If every one in this town comes to

me and says they want me to be sheriff, then I'll consider running for the office. But I'm not going out into the street and try to stop the Arizona Kid. I may not agree with him, but I'm not going to mess with him."

"But the Old Sheriff wants you to run against the Kid," someone says. "You know the Arizona Kid will set Little Elephant Horn back twenty years."

"I know it," Pennsylvania Bill says, "and I'm available. But the only way I can be convinced is if all the townspeople carry me on their shoulders down Main Street."

"Would you consider being deputy sheriff?"

"I'd have to find out where the Arizona Kid stood first, but I wouldn't rule it out."

It's 11:30 and the nervous citizens go over to see former Deputy Sheriff Dick. They plead with him to do something about the Arizona Kid.

Dick says, "Men, I'll do anything any one wants me to—but I ain't going to tangle with the Arizona Kid. If you can knock him off, I'd be very happy to run for sheriff. But I'm not about to get into a fight."

The clock at the railroad station reads 11:45. The citizens go to see the Rock. He tells them he can't stop the Arizona Kid alone. He almost got killed trying.

"I'm willing to go out into the street with a gang of guys and I can supply some guns and horses. But the Arizona Kid has me outnumbered and I can't do it by myself."

It's five of twelve. The responsible citizens hear the train whistle and they all go to their houses, lock the doors, pull down their window shades.

At high noon the Arizona Kid gets off the train as his laughing henchmen cheer. He walks down the main street of Little Elephant Horn prepared to shoot it out with anyone who tries to stop him. But no one dares to come out into the hot noon sun.

The only difference between our film and the original *High Noon* is that in this one nobody wants to play Gary Cooper.

"LIFEBOAT"

There are all these fellows in the lifeboat. There are Nelson, and Bill, and George, and Harold, and Cabot and Dick, and they had been put adrift by Captain Barry and his ruthless crew.

They are rowing to shore to get some help. The lifeboat is creaky and the water is rough.

Dick shouts encouragement: "Don't worry, men, we'll make it!"

"Why don't you row?" Nelson asks him.

"I didn't say I would row," Dick replies.

"Well, if you won't row," Bill says, "you can bail the water out of the boat."

Dick grabs a pail but instead of bailing water out of the boat, he puts more water into it.

"What the hell are you doing?" George says.

"I'm bailing," Dick says.

"No, you're not. You're trying to sink us all," Harold says.

"That's a terrible thing to accuse me of," Dick says. "If it wasn't for me and Ike you wouldn't be in this boat."

Nelson says, "Oh shut up and give us a hand rowing."

Dick grabs an oar but every time the men row forward he rows backward.

Cabot gets angry. "Are you going to row with us or against us?"

"I agreed to row but I didn't say I'd row with you. Did anyone hear me say how I was going to row?"

Bill shouts, "Will you sit down and stop rocking the boat?"

"Don't tell me what to do. You're not the captain of this boat. I've had more experience than you've had. This happens to be my seventh sinking crisis."

The men keep rowing while Dick sits and sulks.

Suddenly Harold shouts, "Sharks! There are sharks all over the place!"

Dick jumps up. "Don't worry, men! I can deal with sharks."

"What are we going to do?" Cabot asks.

"The sharks are hungry. The only way you can get rid of them is to throw somebody in the water."

"You must be out of your mind," Nelson says.

"I'm not out of my mind. Look at it this way. There's six of us in the boat. If we throw one guy over, five of us will be saved. We have to think of the greatest good for the greatest number."

"But who are we going to throw overboard?"

Dick's eyes narrow. "What about it, George? Why don't you make the sacrifice?"

George looks around nervously. "Why does it have to be me?"

"Well, it's got to be somebody."

"I don't want to go."

"Forget the sharks," Bill shouts, "and row. We've still got a chance to stick together."

While the rest of them are rowing Dick sneaks a drink of water from the cask.

Then he shoves half of a loaf of bread under his shirt.

"I've got to think of myself," he mutters. "When they exhaust themselves I'll be captain of the boat and it will be like old times."

The land is still far off and can barely be seen as the sun is setting. The men, weary and thirsty, pull at the oars. Except for Dick, who quietly slips the anchor over the side.

"Come on fellows," he shouts. "Row, row, row."

NOTES FROM THE *ANDREA DORIA*

When you tell someone from the East that you were at the Republican convention in San Francisco, you g   he same reaction as if you told them you were on the An___a Doria.

"What was it really like?" my friends ask, quaking.

"It wasn't too bad," I say, trying to stiffen my upper lip.

"Weren't you frightened?"

"I guess I'd be a liar if I said I wasn't scared, but once I was in the Cow Palace I tried not to think about it."

"What frightened you the most?"

"When Senator Dirksen called Senator Goldwater 'a peddler's grandson.' I didn't know what the reaction of the crowd would be. Dirksen kept repeating it, too. It was really scary."

"What did you think of General Eisenhower's attack on columnists and commentators?"

"Well, I've always said that any one who gives you a column for Thursday can't be all bad."

"Nixon attacked the columnists, too."

"I know and it was very disappointing to me because Nixon has always said he never deals in personalities. One had the feeling in San Francisco that the Republicans were running against the columnists instead of the Democrats."

"Outside of Eisenhower's attack on the columnists, what did you think of his performance there?"

"It was memorable."

"It that all you can say about it?"

Two days later I had moved two miles closer to the farm, but I still had three miles to go. The policeman came back.

"I'll give you a tip. Ike's leaving for California in the morning and you'll never get to see him at this rate. My suggestion is to wait by a railroad crossing and try to talk to him in his private railroad car as he goes by."

I thanked the cop and drove to a crossing near Harrisburg. Two days later Ike went by and I shouted, "Hi, Ike."

The former President gave me one of his big grins and waved with both arms.

If that isn't an endorsement, I don't know what is.

THE MAKING OF A CONSERVATIVE

According to Senator Barry Goldwater there was a grass-roots movement toward conservatism that was sweeping the country. Since I always like to get on the bandwagon early, I dashed over to the Statler Hilton one day to attend a convention of archconservatives and right-wing fellow travelers, sponsored by a weekly newspaper devoted to fighting Communism, Socialism, New Frontierism, Liberal Republicanism, Governor Rockefellerism, and the United States Supreme Court.

I went up to the registration desk on the mezzanine floor and told the man, "Sir, I've been swept up by the grass-roots movement and I'd like to become a conservative. How do I go about it?"

He pinned a BARRY GOLDWATER FOR PRESIDENT button on my necktie and replied, "I'll have to ask you some questions first, to see if you're one of us."

"Yes sir. Ask anything you want. You won't catch me taking the Fifth Amendment."

"Good. How do you feel about the Federal income tax?"

"Lousy, I think it's a scheme by left-wingers in the government to make us pay for socialistic projects such as urban renewal, old age pensions, unemployment insurance, Federal education and welfare payments for illegitimate children. If I had my way I would take the money I paid in income taxes and invest it in the stock market where it belongs."

"Now let me ask you this. Where do you stand on nuclear disarmament?"

"I'm against it. I think we should not only continue testing,

but we should drop a few bombs on other countries to show
the Russians we mean business."

"Very good. What about desegregation?"

"I think desegregation is a Communist conspiracy to mon-
grelize the races, and a violation of the Tenth Amendment
of the United States."

"Would you want your sister to marry a Negro?"

"Yes. But that's because she voted for Johnson, and the
whole family is mad at her."

"How do you feel about fluoridation of water?"

"Fluoridation is a socialistic scheme to contaminate our
drinking water so we'll have less cavities, thus depriving dentists of making money under our American free enterprise
system."

"What do you think of Bobby Kennedy?"

"Boooooooooo."

"How do you feel about the Supreme Court?"

"They should all be impeached," I said. "I say take the
prayers out of the churches and put them back in the schools
where they belong."

"Where do you stand on the United Nations?"

"The United Nations is a Communist organization with the
specific purpose of keeping us out of war. I think U Thant
should be impeached and the United Nations building should
be turned over to Conrad Hilton for a new hotel."

"You seem to be doing very well," the man said.

"Yes sir. I'm not trying to become a conservative for
laughs."

"Let me ask this question. What is your personal opinion
of Dwight Eisenhower?"

"He was a good general but when he became President
he became a Communist and sold us out to the Russians."

"Why do you say he was a good general?" the man said
suspiciously.

"I must have lost my head," I cried.

But it was too late. The man took back the BARRY GOLD-
WATER FOR PRESIDENT button and showed me to the elevator.

"For a moment there," he said, "I thought you were one
of us. But you gave yourself away."

"Give me another chance," I begged.

He shook his head.

"We're a grass-roots movement and we can't afford to take
chances with Eisenhower lovers like you."

A TEST FOR GOLDWATER

Of all the candidates running for the highest office of the land, there was none as outspoken on the issues of the day as Senator Barry Goldwater. No matter what you think of him as Presidential timber, you can't help admiring his courage in saying whatever comes to his mind—or foot.

Last January the good Senator from Arizona said, "I don't feel safe at all about our missiles. I wish the Defense Department could tell the American people how undependable the missiles actually are. . . . I'll probably catch hell for saying it, but our long-range missiles are not dependable at all."

Secretary McNamara immediately reacted to Senator Goldwater's charges, which he said were "completely misleading, politically irresponsible and damaging to national security and supported by no information classified or otherwise."

Now this leaves the average American in one whale of a spot. Who is right, Goldwater or McNamara? How will the public ever know the truth?

There is only one fair way to settle the dispute, and I believe both sides will go along with it. I suggest that Senator Goldwater be placed in a rowboat, somewhere in the middle of the Pacific Ocean, by himself. His exact position would be radioed to an ICBM station on the West Coast. At a signal from Secretary McNamara the ICBM would be fired at Senator Goldwater. If Senator Goldwater escapes getting hit and is able to row back to the United States, he will have proved beyond a shadow of doubt that he was right, and therefore deserves to be President.

But if the ICBM proves to be accurate and hits its target then Senator Goldwater should agree to have his name removed from the primary in New Hampshire.

The big question is whether the Defense Department would be willing to waste a two-million-dollar missile on such a test, particularly when it has pledged itself to an economy drive. The feeling at the Defense Department is that in this case they would.

As a matter of fact several high Defense officials have offered to conduct the test in Senator Goldwater's home state if he doesn't have time to go to the Pacific.

One Defense spokesman said, "Not only would it settle the

ICBM question once and for all, but it would get Senator Goldwater's campaign off the ground."

No one is sure that even if the Defense Department agreed to the test, Senator Goldwater would go along with it. "He refused to debate Governor Rockefeller," a pundit pointed out, "so why would he agree to be shot at by a missile?"

I believe that the pundit is wrong. Senator Goldwater is a man of action, not of words. Anyone who is willing to attack Cuba, withdraw recognition from the Soviet Union, resume nuclear testing and demand a crackdown on Panamanians would certainly be willing to play along with a little old missile shot in the Pacific Ocean.

Besides, the Defense Department has a lot more to lose than Senator Goldwater. If the test fails they'll have to dump all their ICBMs and start from scratch, and Secretary McNamara will look awfully silly.

Senator Goldwater has nothing to lose if the test is a success except possibly the nomination.

I'm well aware this is a pretty farfetched idea, but I'm sure of one thing. I'm certainly going to catch hell for saying it.

DEFOLIATE OR DIE

When Barry Goldwater was interviewed in May, 1964, on television, he suggested that one of the ways of destroying the Viet Cong's supply lines in the jungles was to destroy the foliage with low-yield atomic weapons. "When you remove the foliage, you remove the cover," the Senator was quoted as saying. This, I discovered, is known in military terms as "defoliation."

There were many harsh criticisms of the Goldwater suggestion, not because it was considered reckless, but because most Americans were astonished to read you could kill foliage with atomic bombs.

If the government knows of ways to eliminate growth with nuclear weapons, most homeowners feel they should be made available to us rather than shipped to a foreign country.

All of us who have been fighting the battle of crabgrass, weeds, and dandelions have been waiting for some major breakthrough in the destruction of foliage. The military, it appears, had the answer all the time, and if it weren't for Senator Goldwater we would have never known about it.

Of course, low-yield atomic weapons for home use must be

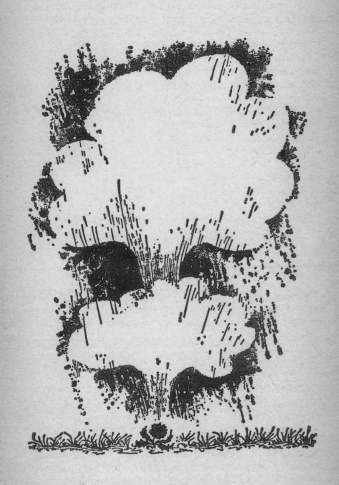

handled very carefully. If not applied correctly, you might knock down your house at the time you're trying to kill your crabgrass.

Or you might destroy weeds in your own garden, but the fallout might injure perfectly good plants in your neighbor's backyard. Sometimes, if not used correctly, atomic weapons can be as dangerous as DDT.

I believe the best way to handle the defoliation program in the United States is to set up a Home User's Service under the Atomic Energy Commission. (If Congress complains that this is another example of government control, the AEF could license low-yield atomic weapons to mail-order houses.)

When the foliage in your backyard gets too great, you could call the Defoliation Service, which would send out an experienced crew to take care of the matter. They could either set off the atomic weapon by detonator or, in the case of larger lawns, drop a low-yield bomb from an airplane.

To do the job properly you would need cooperation from your neighbors. Despite the great strides that have been made in defoliation, you still may have two to three days of fallout, and so your neighbors would have to agree to stay in their cellars until all your crabgrass was dead.

Since it is still in the experimental stage, there may be instances where the atomic weapon could be too strong for the foliage, and this could make everyone's garden in the area uninhabitable for several weeks. But you can't have an omelet if you don't break an egg and you certainly can't have a good-looking backyard if you don't experiment with new types of weed killers.

I feel Senator Goldwater did a great disservice to this country by suggesting we defoliate Vietnam when there is so much unwanted foliage right here in the United States.

Anyone in his right mind knows defoliation begins at home.

THEY'RE AT IT AGAIN

The League of Women Voters was at it again. They were trying to get women to vote in November. As one of the founders of the Bull Moose Party, which had been working quietly for the repeal of the 19th Amendment (we were the first to point out that women can't cook—96.4 percent of all professional chefs are men; women can't sew—39 percent of all couturiers are men; women can't even have babies without help—92.7 percent of all babies are delivered by men), I have posed the question: "Why should women have the right to vote if they can't do the things they're supposed to do?"

New evidence was unearthed to show that the Bull Moose Party was not just whistling "Dixie." A book written by Dr. L. P. Brockett, entitled *Women's Rights, Wrongs and Privileges,* has become to the Bull Moose Party what the Blue Book is to the John Birch Society. Writing in 1869, Dr. Brockett spelled out the many disadvantages there were in giving the franchise to women.

Dr. Brockett maintained that women were well represented in politics by their husbands and fathers. No reasonable request made by a woman through their menfolk went unheeded. As Dr. Brockett put it, "The general sentiment of tenderness and regard for the female sex on the part of men both in high and low station is their greatest protection and safeguard, and they would lose this if they voted themselves."

The good doctor pointed out that letting women vote was against the natural order of things.

"When a husband and father votes, he is voting for the family, but if women are allowed to vote they would be voting as individuals, which is incompatible with the organization of society and subversive to its best interests."

Give the women the right to vote, Dr. Brockett warned, and the male voter will say, "I have no need to consider anybody's interest but my own."

Dr. Brockett believed, and his prophecies have borne fruit, that once a woman was given the vote the sexes would be at war. He wrote, "Let man understand that woman is determined to stand for herself and neither desires nor needs his assistance, then an antagonism would be engendered which many waters could not quench."

He pointed out that if a woman disagreed politically with her husband it could lead to separation and even permanent estrangement.

"Women allow their passions to get overheated and call it righteous sentiment. They make more of their idols, raise more false halos about them, and even have it as a kind of virtue to bear defeat badly in their cause. There is no hatred so implacable, especially with women, as political hatred, no bitterness so intense as that which is engendered by political strife."

And how could you hide these passions? Dr. Brockett predicted that if women got the vote their charm and beauty would disappear and "women will acquire a more careworn expression; they will have a sharper, more wiry voice, modulated upon a higher key; and that 'lean and hungry look' which has been characteristic of politicians since the time of Cassius."

The doctor dwelt on the fact that if good women got suffrage they would have to go down to the polls and stand in line with servant women, women of the lower classes, and even women of ill repute whom, he predicted, would be paid to be there early.

As everyone knows, Brockett's words weren't heeded and women did get the vote. All his predictions have come true. The only hope to bring us back to the good old days was Barry Goldwater, but unless Senator Goldwater called for the repeal of the 19th Amendment, the Bull Moose Party was going to sit this one out.

HOW HUBERT WAS CHOSEN

Little by little the story is being revealed as to how President Johnson chose Senator Hubert Humphrey as his running mate. I now can tell the whole story.

In the beginning all the polls indicated that, no matter who Johnson ran with, he would lose votes. So he decided to run alone. But he needed a legal ruling on it. So he called the Attorney General, Robert Kennedy, and said, "Bobby, can you tell me if Ah need a Vice-Presidential candidate on the ticket?"

Mr. Kennedy said, "Yes, sir, I'm afraid you do."

"That's a shame. You don't have any suggestions, do you?"

"I haven't given it much thought, sir."

"Well, if you can come up with somebody, let me know."

The following weeks it is known that the President talked to everyone concerning the Vice-Presidency. He sought the advice of Senators, Congressmen, businessmen and Governors.

Every once in a while he wandered over to the White House fence and asked a tourist whom he thought it should be. It was a big decision and he hated to make it alone.

As time went on the list got longer. He let it be known that 67 Senators, 24 Governors, 134 Congressmen, 50 women and 12 Secret Service men were being considered seriously for the office.

And every day he called up Bobby Kennedy and said, "You come up with a name, Bobby?"

"I'm racking my brain, sir, but I just can't think of anybody."

The President conferred with intimates in Texas, close newspaper friends, Pentagon officials and his accounting firm of Haskins and Sells. They all had suggestions and President Johnson wrote down every one. The list had been extended to include 136 mayors, 230 state legislators, 590 county chairmen, and everyone who had contributed more than a thousand dollars to the Democratic National Committee.

He called up Mr. Kennedy again. "Bobby, it's getting near the time. Ah sure could use your help in this matter."

Bobby said, "Mr. President, I'm stuck. You need a young man who's held important government office, is known to the American public, has traveled abroad, and has a large political machine behind him. I don't know where we can find him."

"Well, keep trying," the President said.

For weeks a steady stream of potential candidates visited the President's office. Each one in turn was assured that when the final decision was made he would be the man. Unknown to all of them the President had added the Washington telephone book to his list of prospects.

But he was still depending on Bobby Kennedy to come up with a man.

Then two weeks before the convention the President heard Postmaster General Gronouski had told a friend jokingly he wouldn't mind the Vice-Presidential spot. The President hates to be pushed, so he eliminated his entire Cabinet from the race.

Up until convention time the President still had no idea whom he wanted to give the job to. Then one day, while he was eating lunch with Mrs. Johnson, she said to him, "You know, Lyndon, we owe the Hubert Humphreys a dinner."

The President said, "Ah don't have time to have dinner with the Humphreys, but Ah tell you what, Lady Bird, Ah'll make it up to them some way."

FROM GOLDWATER WITH LOVE

On the Goldwater Special leaving from Washington for its whistle-stop tour I found the train filled with the candidate, his staff, and 115 mysterious people all of whom claimed to be newspapermen. It was raining and cold and dark and I knew something was going to happen.

I didn't have to wait long. A knock sounded on my compartment door. I reached for my Olivetti. I opened the door slowly and suddenly I saw her. A beautiful brunette, tall but not too tall, round but not too round, soft but not too soft, rushed in.

"You've got to help me," she cried.

"Name it," I said, helping her into the compartment.

"They're after me," she said.

"Who is?"

"The Goldwater people," she said, shaking with fear.

"Why?" I asked as I poured her out a glass of brandy.

"They think I'm a Democrat," she said. "You see, I was on my way to see my mother in Marietta, Ohio, and I got on the wrong train. Someone has been passing out anti-Goldwater literature and they think it's me."

Before I could answer, there was a knock on the door.

"What do you want?" I said, reaching for my Olivetti again.

"We're looking for a beautiful brunette," a Goldwater aide shouted.

"What does she look like?" I yelled through the door.

"She's tall, but not too tall, round but not too round, soft but not too soft."

"Sorry, I haven't seen her," I said.

"Who's that in there with you?" someone demanded.

"My sister."

They went away.

The brunette threw her arms around me.

"How can I ever thank you?"

I thought and thought, but I couldn't come up with any ideas.

"You stay here," I told her. "I'm going back to the bar car and find out what's going on. Don't answer the door until you hear three knocks and then say, 'Extremism in the pursuit of liberty,' and I'll reply, 'Is no vice.'"

I went to the bar car where the search for the brunette was going on in earnest.

The Goldwater people were frantic. "No one can leave the train," an aide shouted, "until the suspect is found."

Since we were moving at 60 miles an hour everyone agreed. I bought a couple of sandwiches and went back to my compartment. I forgot the password and walked right in. There she was on the floor working a tiny mimeograph machine which kept repeating, "In your head you know he's wrong."

"You lied to me," I screamed, grabbing her arm.

"Sure, I lied to you," she snarled. "I'm a Democratic spy and I'm glad I did it."

"I'm going to have to turn you in," I said.

She put her arms around me and whispered in my ear, "Why? In your heart you know I'm right."

I was about to ring for a porter when the thought occurred to me: "What the hell. This is Goldwater's problem."

IN OUR HEARTS

There has been a great deal of soul-searching and name-calling amongst Republicans since the Presidential election. Dean Burch, Chairman of the Republican National Committee, Barry Goldwater and Bill Miller all have come under heavy attack for the campaign they waged and moderate Republicans have demanded their ouster.

Strangely enough, the only people who seem to be defending the Goldwater campaign are the Democrats. We were having lunch at the National Democratic Club the other day and one of the leaders of the Democratic party told us, "I think Dean Burch has been unfairly attacked for the campaign he waged. We believe he did a great job and we hope he stays in for another four years."

"But didn't he make a lot of mistakes?"

"None that we can think of. We were very satisfied with everything he did. Of course, we were sorry to lose those five states in the South, but we can't hold Burch responsible for that."

"What about Barry Goldwater?"

"Here again, we feel people are being too critical. Mr. Goldwater made a great contribution to the Democratic Party and I know he'll be remembered for it for many years to come."

"Is that true of Bill Miller, too?"

"It certainly is. Bill Miller is one of our favorites, and since the election is over, I haven't heard one Democrat utter a harsh word against him."

"Then you think Governor Rockefeller was wrong in criticizing the campaign the two Republican candidates waged?"

"I can't speak for Rockefeller. All I can say is that as far as the Democrats are concerned the Republicans couldn't have picked two better men than Goldwater and Miller."

"You don't think they made political mistakes?"

"Every one makes mistakes during a campaign. We would have liked to have seen Goldwater hit the nuclear war issue harder, and perhaps attack the Social Security system with more vigor, but you can't have everything. He did the best he could with what he had and we wouldn't have changed one word of any of his speeches."

"It's nice to hear some kind words about Goldwater and Miller these days."

"You won't hear any one in this club knocking them. As a matter of fact, we hope they run again in 1968 and we're going to do everything we can to see the Republicans don't make any changes. Every Democratic club in the country has sent a telegram supporting Dean Burch and the entire Barry Goldwater team. You can say what you want, the Democrats are not the kind to desert a loser."

"Have you told Mr. Goldwater about it?"

"We've tried to, but he won't answer his phone. I guess he was afraid we were going to be critical of him. But if he knew how much we thought of him, particularly with all the carping going on in his own party, I think he would have been pleased. In our Democratic hearts, we know he will always be right."

THE TURNCOAT

I have a friend who has four children. He is an ardent Democrat and worked hard for President Johnson's election. My friend's wife and three of his children were also for Mr. Johnson. But his nine-year-old daughter happened to be for Senator Goldwater.

"At first," he told me, "I thought it was amusing. But I don't think it's very funny anymore. How would you like it if you came home after a hard day's work and instead of your daughter kissing you she shouted, 'Hooray for Goldwater!'?"

"Why is she doing it?" I asked him.

"I can't figure it out. She's a good child, we've always lavished love and affection on her, and she doesn't get punished more than any other kid. But somewhere along the way we must have failed."

"Has she told you her reasons for supporting Goldwater?"

"No. Every time I ask her, she just giggles and shouts, 'Hooray for Goldwater!' Lately she's been wearing Goldwater buttons on her dress and somebody in the neighborhood has been slipping her Goldwater stickers which she pastes up around the house, and it's driving me nuts. Look, I want my kid to grow up and think for herself, but she doesn't have to start with Goldwater."

"Have you tried to discuss the issues with her?"

"Of course I have. I told her that if Goldwater was elected he would make all children go to school on Saturdays and he would do away with summer vacations. He also was advocating an hour's extra homework each night and was supporting daily tests in arithmetic."

"Didn't that scare her?"

"It did for a couple of days, but then the Goldwater people got to her and told her President Johnson was going to cut all children's allowances, close down candy stores, and abolish bubble gum."

"What was your response to that?"

"I told her Goldwater was going to put a tax on all bicycles, doll houses, and doll clothes. I warned her if Goldwater was elected she would have to take care of her baby sister every afternoon, and he would forbid anyone under twenty-one from watching television."

"I should think that would have done it."

"It would have except that she went back to the Goldwater neighbors and they told her President Johnson was against the Three Stooges, sand piles, and Disneyland."

"I didn't think the campaign was going to become this rough," I said.

"I wouldn't mind if it was just her, but she's enlisted three of her friends in the campaign. How would you like to be a registered Democrat and have a Goldwater cell in your basement?"

"What does your wife have to say about this?"

"She thinks it's part of the parent backlash. My wife believes we should pretend to be for Goldwater and then our daughter would be for Johnson."

"Why don't you do it?"

"I'm afraid of losing the other three kids. They might think we really are for Goldwater."

"You do have a problem."

"The worst part of it is I've lost all perspective. When she's bad I don't know if I'm punishing her for her behavior or because she's for Goldwater. It makes me feel guilty as hell."

"Why don't you tell her the Beatles are going to vote for Johnson?"

"Say," he shouted happily, "I never thought of that!"

c. The Voter
★★★★★★★★★★★

HE WANTED TO VOTE

If there is anybody who gets me mad, it's somebody who wants to vote after a computer has declared a winner in a nationally televised election.

Last June one night, only 23 minutes after they were on the air, and 48 minutes before the polls were closed, the Columbia Broadcasting System declared Senator Goldwater the winner in the California primary. While only 2 percent of the returns were in, it was sufficient, as far as the network was concerned, to declare a winner.

As soon as I heard the results, I telephoned a friend of mine who lives in San Francisco.

He said, "I can't speak to you now. I have to go out and vote. I've only got 40 minutes left."

"But haven't you heard?" I said. "CBS has declared Goldwater the winner. There is no sense in bothering to vote now."

"Gee, I hadn't heard. It's official, huh?"

"As far as the computers are concerned it is. Any one who votes now is just wasting his time."

"But maybe I ought to vote anyway. After all, I did register."

I got angry. "Are you trying to make a monkey out of Walter Cronkite? I told you the vote profile analysis gave the primary to Goldwater."

"What's the vote profile analysis?"

"Well, they take a Buddhist in San Pedro, a Mexican in Los Angeles, and a hod carrier in San Francisco, and find out how they voted. They put it on a card and in a few seconds they know who the Presidential candidate will be."

"Then my vote doesn't have any meaning?" he said.

"Well, I wouldn't say that. It's an American custom to vote and, although it's gone out of style with electronics, people still like to do it to remind them of the good old days. They call it a raw vote on TV."

"What's a raw vote?"

"It's an uncooked vote. No one has run it up the flagpole or put it on the train to Westport, if you know what I mean. It's sort of anticlimactic. The CBS television commentators refer to the raw vote with a certain amount of contempt, but some people are still curious about it."

My friend said, "What would happen if I voted now?"

"I believe CBS would get very mad. They have all their figures in and I don't think they'd appreciate it if you loused them up."

"I think I'll still vote."

"That's a pretty crummy thing to do," I said. "CBS has put a lot of money into their vote profile analysis and computing machines. They've hired some of the best pollsters in the business to give us an accurate forecast on this primary. I don't see why you should go out at this hour and try to change the results. Remember, CBS has a lot more at stake in this election than you have."

"I guess you're right. They are experts and I'm just one voter. I'm sorry I thought I could change anything."

"It's not your fault," I told him. "Lots of people think they can still beat the machines, but they're finding out they can't. To paraphrase Abraham Lincoln, this nation, under CBS, shall have a new birth of freedom—and the government of the computers, by the computers, and for the computers shall not perish from the earth."

THE BALLYHOO GETS TO HIM

The big question asked at a political convention is whether all the spontaneous demonstrations, the parades and the colorful ballyhoo have any effect on changing the delegates' votes.

The answer is an unqualified yes.

I spoke to an uncommitted Republican delegate who told me he would have no idea whom to vote for if it weren't for the demonstrations that preceded the nominations.

He said, "I'm not concerned with issues. I'm interested only in personalities. I think the one who puts on the best spontaneous demonstrations has earned the nomination."

"How do you judge them?"

"Well, I like girls. I've always believed that the candidate who has the prettiest girls working for him is probably the one who can do the best job for our country. The first thing I do when I come to the convention is to take a look at the girls."

"Is there anything special you look for?"

"Oh, I look to see the way they're dressed. If they have a neat appearance. If they smile when they talk to you. Important things like that."

"Is there anything else that influences your vote?"

"A good band during a demonstration can always move me. I like a lot of trombones in a band. In 1952 I was going to vote for Taft, but he was weak on trombones, so I went over to Eisenhower."

"What are some of the other factors that affect your vote?"

"Did I tell you about girls?"

"Yes, you did."

"Well, let's see. I always look to see who has the most colorful posters. I look for originality in posters as well as size. It isn't enough just to have the poster show the candidate's face. The same goes for buttons. I always felt Nixon lost in 1960 because his buttons didn't say anything."

"What about spontaneous demonstrations?" I asked.

"I think they're almost as important as girls. As a matter of fact, I never decide which way to go until I see the spontaneous demonstrations. A convention is much too serious a business to make up your mind before you see how a candidate has organized his demonstration. I think that's where Harold Stassen makes his mistake every time. He never seems to be able to get his spontaneous demonstrations off the ground."

"I hear Goldwater is very strong on spontaneous demonstrations."

"That's what I hear, too, and I'm really looking forward to seeing it. Scranton probably started too late to organize a good spontaneous demonstration, but I'm keeping an open mind."

"What else do you use as a yardstick?"

"Well, there are the girls."

"You mentioned them."

"That's probably it, then. Of course, if someone wants to buy me a drink, I'll take that into account, too."

"Do you ever try to find out where the candidates stand?" He looked at me as if I was crazy. "What for?"

WHAT HE DOESN'T KNOW

The political poll has become one of the biggest factors in American politics. From now on until Election Day political pollsters will be traversing the length and breadth of the United States, questioning people on their feelings toward the candidates and issues of the day.

It is interesting to note that in every poll there are a certain percentage of people who are "undecided," "don't know" or are "not sure" of any of the questions. Who are these people? What do they believe in? How do they think?

In order to find out, I decided to take a poll of my own and interview the president of the UDKNS Society.

I rang the bell and he came to the door. "Sir, I'm taking a survey of the Undecided, Don't Know, Not Sure Society. Could you give me some information?"

"How many members are in your society?"

"I'm not sure about that," he replied.

"Well, how often do you meet?"

"I don't really know."

"What does the organization stand for?"

"We're undecided as of this moment."

"Why did you form such a society?"

"I hesitate to answer that. My guess would be we started it because there were so many people in this country who were undecided on so many issues that we felt they should be represented. In any poll, if you multiply us, we could run into the millions."

"How do you qualify for the organization?"

"By NOT having any convictions and by sticking to them. We study each question carefully and then decide we don't know the answer."

"It sounds difficult."

"It isn't easy these days, particularly with all the communications around us. Most of us try not to read newspapers or watch news programs on television. We never discuss politics at home and we stay out of bars because you usually have to take sides there."

"When you do meet, what do you talk about?"

"Nothing much. We have only one rule. If anyone expresses an opinion on anything, he's asked to resign."

"But, sir, what value does your organization have if it doesn't stand for anything?"

"We have more value than anybody else. Nobody cares who is for or against something. It's the 'undecided' that the candidates are worried about. They spend more time and money on us than anybody. We count for something in an election year."

"But when do the undecided people make up their minds?"

"I have no idea. Once they've decided, we're no longer interested in them."

"Well, thank you very much, sir."

"Don't mention it. I'm not sure whether I should have talked to you. I don't know if I've made a mistake giving you all this information and I'm undecided whether you should print it or not. But if you don't use my name, I guess it will be all right."

PSYCHOLOGICAL WARFARE

Nobody likes to talk about it, but there is a great deal of stress during a Presidential election on psychological political warfare.

Both sides are great at spreading rumors about the enemy and using any possible tactic to destroy the other.

I have a friend, a staunch Democrat, who, every Presidential election year, claims he wins hundreds of votes for his side by a very simple maneuver. "Every time I take a taxi, I tip the driver five cents and say, 'Vote Republican!' "

Another Democratic friend spends his spare time driving around Washington, cutting off people, honking his horn at them, and stealing their parking places. He does this in a car that has GOLDWATER FOR PRESIDENT stickers all over it.

"I don't know if I'm accomplishing much now," he told me, "but I think I'll pick up most of my votes in late October when I accidentally stall on the 14th Street bridge."

A Republican friend has a gimmick that he says works miracles. He picks people's names out of the phone book and calls them up at midnight and says, "I'm a volunteer for Johnson. Would you have a few minutes to talk to me?"

A Republican acquaintance claims he won many votes for Nixon in 1960 by scattering Democratic campaign literature on his neighbor's lawns. He hopes to do it again for Goldwater this year.

A Democrat I know says his mother, who has never been active in politics before, is so upset about Senator Goldwater's nomination that she is working day and night for his defeat.

"What does she do?" I asked.

"She walks around in old tennis shoes with a Goldwater button on her chest, insulting all the merchants in Georgetown."

"That's not bad. But what have you been doing?"

"Not much so far," he admitted. "My only contribution is that every time I go to a party I put on a Goldwater button and start making passes at all the independents' wives.

"My brother, on the other hand, has been doing very well getting hostesses to vote for Johnson."

"How does he do that?"

"Every time he goes to a dinner party he announces loudly that he's for Goldwater and then spills wine on the hostess's new tablecloth."

He told me: "It's going to be a very tough fight. We have a woman neighbor, a Goldwater supporter, who calls up doctors and dentists and asks them if they have any new information on President Johnson's plan for socialized medicine."

One greeting card company is now printing up a letter on Republican stationery which you can send to a friend, informing him that his house has been selected for a neighborhood fund-raising drive and he can expect 50 Republican neighbors to show up for a barbecue, "weather permitting."

As the campaign gets hotter, psychological political warfare will be used more and more to attract the undecided vote.

While most people abhor this type of campaigning, a specialist in psychological political planning told me, "Extremism in the pursuit of voters is no vice."

THE BITTER YEAR

Election years are very tough on the American public, and great cause for bitterness. People you thought you could trust turn out to be bigoted, stupid, narrow-minded and uninformed. Friends turn against friends, fathers turn against sons, daughters turn against their mothers.

This particular election year of 1964 was one of the bitterest of all, if my own family is any example.

My Uncle Leo wasn't talking to my Uncle Charlie since he found out Uncle Charlie was for Senator Goldwater. Uncle Leo said that Uncle Charlie wanted to get us into a war. Uncle Charlie denied the charge and said he was for fiscal responsibility, and he suspected that Uncle Leo was a Socialist. Uncle Leo said Uncle Charlie was probably a John Bircher.

In the meantime my Cousin Sarah refused to invite Uncle Leo over to her house because Uncle Leo was mad at General Eisenhower for not speaking out against Senator Goldwater. Cousin Sarah was not for Barry Goldwater but she felt Uncle Leo should have more respect for General Eisenhower. Sarah's husband, on the other hand, was mad at Uncle Charlie because he claimed Uncle Charlie shot from the hip and didn't think things through.

Aunt Pauline happened to be for Governor Rockefeller and got into a big fight with Aunt Ruth because Aunt Ruth said Rockefeller drove the Republicans into the Goldwater camp by getting a divorce. Aunt Pauline said that Aunt Ruth had a narrow mind about politics and should have kept her big mouth shut.

Uncle Sidney was banned from Aunt Molly's house because, although Uncle Sidney is a registered Republican, he announced at the family Fourth of July picnic that he was going to vote for President Johnson.

Aunt Molly called him a carpetbagger. Uncle Sidney told Aunt Molly she didn't even know what the word carpetbagger meant, so Aunt Molly said he couldn't come into her house.

In the meantime at the same Fourth of July party, Uncle Charlie announced that if President Johnson won the election he was moving to Canada. Uncle Leo said he'd give him a farewell party, which didn't go over very big with Uncle Charlie, who didn't think anyone would take him up on it.

To make matters worse, Aunt Augusta said she wasn't going to invite Uncle Lou and Aunt Stella to Cousin Alice's wedding because Uncle Lou wanted Bobby Kennedy for Vice-President. Aunt Stella was furious because she invited Aunt Augusta to her daughter's wedding even though Aunt Augusta voted for Nixon.

There was a small pro-Scranton group in the family but they hadn't picked up any supporters since Governor Scranton announced he was going to run.

And we were all mad at Cousin Marvin because he paid a hundred dollars to go to a fund-raising dinner for President Johnson, when he owed everyone in the family money.

Cousin Marvin said if he hadn't gone to the dinner he would have lost his job with the government.

And so it went. The next few months were tough ones for my family, as they probably were for families all over the country. It was probably the only time in our lives when water was thicker than blood.

NEW YORK EXPLAINED

There was no doubt that Bobby Kennedy would have a tough time running for Senator from New York State. There were so many things he would have to learn in such a short span of time.

I can imagine what was going on at a Kennedy strategy meeting.

The Kennedy campaign group was gathered around a large map of New York and Stephen Smith was briefing Mr. Kennedy.

"Now, Bobby," he said using a pointer, "this is the Hudson River over here and this is the East River."

"Say, that would make Manhattan an island then, wouldn't it?" Mr. Kennedy said.

"Exactly, but you must remember New York City has four other boroughs."

"I think I know them. There's the Bronx, Brooklyn, Queens, and . . ."

"It's another island."

"Let me concentrate. I did know it."

"It starts with S," Mr. Smith said.

"I've got it! Staten Island," Mr. Kennedy said.

"Very good," Mr. Smith said.

"What's that land mass over there on the other side of the Hudson?"

"That is New Jersey. We don't have to worry about that place."

"It looks easier to get to than Staten Island," Mr. Kennedy said.

"Well, forget about it. This is Fifth Avenue. It divides the East Side from the West Side."

"Hey, that's a good idea," Mr. Kennedy agreed.

He studied the map for a few moments. "Where's the Common?"

"There is no Common in New York," Mr. Smith explained. "Over here is Central Park."

"I get it. Is that where the Red Sox play?"

"They're not called the Red Sox, Bobby. They're called the Yankees," Mr. Smith said. "And they play at Yankee Stadium.

"The New York Mets, which is the other baseball team, play at Shea Stadium," Mr. Smith added.

"You mean New York's got two baseball teams?"

"That's correct," Mr. Smith said, "and from now on you'll be rooting for both of them."

"Fair enough. Clue me in on football."

"In New York City we have Columbia University."

"I know Columbia," Mr. Kennedy said. "Harvard used to kill them in football."

"Try not to mention that if you can, Bobby."

"I get you. What's that long cape sticking out there?"

"That's not a cape. It's Long Island, and there are a lot of votes out there."

"Long Island. That's a funny name for a cape."

"Now, let's talk about some of the cultural aspects of the city. This is Lincoln Center," Mr. Smith said.

"That's where the Pops Orchestra plays, right?"

"There is no Pops Orchestra in New York, Bobby. It's called the Philharmonic."

"I'll be darned."

"When do I start eating baked beans?" Mr. Kennedy asked.

"You don't eat baked beans in New York, Bobby. You eat bagels."

"Are they anything like baked beans?"

"No, Bobby. A bagel is a hard roll. I think that's enough for today. We'll work on Westchester tomorrow."

GOODBYE, MR. ZILCH

Not everyone wants to win an election. On a lecture date in a Southern city I heard about a fellow named Zilch. It seems that Zilch was a born politician and had run for every kind of office in the country for the past 26 years. Zilch was always defeated, but this didn't bother him at all.

The reason was that Zilch wasn't interested in winning. He was more interested in raising money for his campaign. Zilch might raise between $5,000 and $10,000 to run for office. By being careful in his expenditures and making sure he didn't do anything foolish, Zilch managed to keep 90 percent of the money for himself. This kept him going until the next election rolled around.

Zilch ran for Sheriff, he ran for Mayor, he ran for Coroner, and he ran for Congressman. There was no office he would refuse to run for, providing he raised enough money to support himself and get in some fishing on the side.

Of course, some people who supported Zilch were discouraged by his lackluster campaigns, and a few even complained that they would like to see a few more billboards with Zilch's name on them, but he would always retort he had no funds for outdoor advertising and he didn't have money to throw around like his opponent.

The truth of the matter was that Zilch's opponents were usually his best source of campaign funds.

They knew he didn't have the "will to win," and it was easier to run against Zilch than anybody else in the county. By contributing to Zilch's campaign they were assured of winning an election.

But there happened to be a group of businessmen in the town who were pretty sore at Zilch. They had all contributed at one time or another to Zilch's election campaigns and felt they had not been given value for their money.

So they decided to do something about it. This year Zilch was running for President of the City Council. His opponent, a lawyer, had contributed heavily to Zilch's campaign, knowing Zilch had no intention of winning. In no time at all Zilch had a campaign kitty of $12,000 and he was planning on taking a trip to Europe as soon as he lost and the election was over.

But he hadn't reckoned with the disgruntled businessmen in his town. They came up with a plan. They got together a secret fund and, without Zilch's knowledge or permission, they started plastering ZILCH FOR COUNCILMAN billboards all over town. They distributed thousands of bumper stickers with Zilch's name on them. School children were given Zilch buttons, the local radio stations turned out Zilch commercials.

Zilch was panic-stricken. His opponents felt he had double-crossed them and they were furious. Zilch tried to explain he had nothing to do with the campaign and he hadn't spent a dime on himself. The crowning blow came when a postcard was sent out showing Zilch shaking hands with President Johnson (faked, of course, by Zilch's secret backers).

In a special election and despite his protests that he didn't want the office and had never met Johnson, Zilch won by a landslide.

Zilch is now the unhappiest man in town, not only because he has to work in an elected office, but because he knows his opponents will never contribute to another Zilch campaign. Why should they when Zilch can never be trusted again?

TAKE A LOSER TO LUNCH

The 1964 election is over, and once again it is time to mend fences and make up to the people who happened to be on the other side.

It behooves each winner to search his heart and find words of solace for the loser.

In 1960 I made a plea to those who had voted for Richard Nixon not to leave the United States. As you recall, 90 percent of all Republicans said they would leave the country if Mr. Nixon didn't get in. Most of these people said they would go to Canada, which had the Canadian immigration authorities worried sick.

But fortunately most of the people who vowed to leave the United States thought it over and decided to stick it out.

This year I have heard many Goldwater supporters vow they would not stay in the country if President Johnson got elected, and once again the Canadian government has requested that people reconsider their threats.

"If the polls are right," a Canadian immigration officer told me, "we could wind up with 20 million Republicans moving to Canada this year, and we just can't handle them."

"But most Goldwater supporters have said they can't live in the United States under Johnson and Humphrey."

"We're in sympathy with them, but why don't they go to Argentina?"

In order to help Canada, I believe it is up to everyone to persuade the losing side to remain in the United States.

There are many things that could be done.

One would be to proclaim a "Take a Loser to Lunch Week." During this week the winners would take the losers to the restaurant of their choice. While the losers were eating, the winners could explain to them where the losers made their biggest mistakes. This would bind the wounds and bring the winners and losers closer together again.

Another way to help would be for a winner's family to pay a call on a loser's family and distribute baskets of food, toys, and clean secondhand clothing. The winner could explain the reason for the charity was that the loser had predicted the country would go to blazes if Johnson got in, and therefore the loser could probably use the gifts.

If they wanted to make a community effort, I think the winners could throw a huge post-election barbecue for the losers in the town square. Each winner would be assigned a loser, and he would be responsible for making him happy.

He could present the loser with a Texas sombrero and any Johnson-Humphrey buttons he had left over from the campaign.

He could teach the loser the words to "Hello, Lyndon" and read him excerpts from Johnson speeches. The trick would be to make the loser forget all about the election.

Of course there was always the outside chance that Barry Goldwater might have won the election. In this case there would have been 80 million people wanting to go to Canada. The Canadians seemed to have more to lose in this election than anybody.

II. ON THE BRINK
OF PEACE
☆☆☆☆☆☆☆☆☆☆☆☆☆

WHO'S ON FIRST BASE?

A few weeks ago the U. S. Navy announced that it was trying to perfect a flying submarine which it needed badly to protect the United States. This brought an immediate reaction from the U. S. Air Force, which announced it would soon develop an underseas airplane.

The exchange pointed out the great competition now going on between the armed services and no one is quite sure how it will all come out.

With modern warfare becoming so complicated no one knows what role each of the services should play. At a recent top-secret meeting at the Pentagon some of the questions were thrashed out. It went something like this.

General Patent of the U. S. Army opened the meeting by saying, "Gentlemen, I am happy to announce that the United States Army now has the largest number of airplanes of any armed service in the world."

General Wings of the Air Force shouted, "I protest. The Air Force should have most of the airplanes under its command. We're not going to take this lying down."

Admiral Bilge of the U. S. Navy said, "Speaking of lying down, the U. S. Marine Corps has developed a new helicopter tank which will do away with the necessity of heavy armored divisions. The tank can be flown off aircraft carriers."

General Patent said, "Oh yeh, wise guy. Well the Army has come up with a floating rocket launcher which makes the naval destroyer obsolete."

General Wings pounded the table. "I'd like to get back to these Army aircraft. There is no reason to have Army aircraft."

General Patent replied, "The function of the Air Force is to man Intercontinental Ballistic Missiles underneath the ground. Our airplanes are used to support our troops. The planes you have are too fast for that and you know it."

General Wings pulled some papers out of his briefcase. "We are now building slower planes to operate with our paratroop division."

General Patent said, "What paratroop division?"

"The paratroop division we're forming to protect our Intercontinental Ballistic Missiles."

"The hell you say, Wings. The Army has the responsibility of protecting our ICBMs."

"Not anymore it doesn't."

Admiral Bilge piped up. "Will you two stop fighting? By the time you settle the argument the Navy will have enough Polaris missiles to make the ICBM unnecessary."

General Wings replied, "That's all well and good but when the Air Force gets its own cruisers . . ."

Admiral Bilge said, "What do you mean, cruisers?"

"We have to have our own cruisers to launch our atomic artillery shells!"

"What are you doing with atomic artillery?" General Patent demanded.

"We don't have to tell you everything," General Wings said.

General Patent made a dive for General Wings. Admiral Bilge picked up a water pitcher and threw it at both of them.

Fortunately at that moment the Secretary of Defense walked into the room and after each man explained his position, the Secretary fed this information into a computer and after digesting the facts the computer tape came out with this message: "If I were you I'd close down the Pentagon."

GENERALS ON THE HILL

There has been a lot of criticism over the fact that many Senators and Representatives hold high ranks in the military reserves. Barry Goldwater, for example, is an Air Force major general, commands the 9,999th Air Reserve Squadron, which includes Senator Howard Cannon as a brigadier general and Hawaii's Senator Hiram Fong as a colonel as well as 70 Congressional staffers. Senator Strom Thurmond holds the rank of major general in the Army and he commands an Army

Reserve unit of 90 men on Capitol Hill; Representative William S. Maillard of California is captain of the 75-man Navy unit, which includes Marine Colonel George A. Smathers of Florida.

Critics of the reserve system insist that these members of Congress are no more than a high-powered lobby for their respective services and their only function is to get appropriations for the outfits whose uniforms they wear.

I would like to defend these reserve officers because I feel they have been unjustly vilified. Unfortunately, for security reasons, they cannot defend themselves. But I am under no such wraps.

Each reserve unit at the Capitol has a definite military function far and above lobbying for its particular service.

For example, the 9,999th Air Reserve Squadron has an important role to play in the defense of our country. It is not generally known, but underneath the Capitol in specially constructed hangars are 36 F-105 fighter planes. If anyone ever pushes the button, the entire back lawn of the Capitol will be rolled back and the fighter planes will be brought to the surface.

In the meantime, General Goldwater and members of the 9,999th Air Reserve Squadron will be helped into their flight suits by Senate page boys and will report to the Senate Judiciary Room for a briefing. After being briefed, they will rush to their planes and take off up Constitution Avenue by twos. The primary role of the 9,999th Squadron is to protect the Army-Navy Country Club from attack by unfriendly aircraft.

They will also be assigned to fly cover for any Senators and Representatives who would like to leave Washington in a hurry. And thirdly, they will in all likelihood be allowed to strafe Bobby Baker's home in Spring Valley.

While General Goldwater's planes are in the air, General Strom Thurmond of the U. S. Army Reserve will dig in on the Virginia side of the Potomac to make sure no Negroes are served in segregated restaurants during the emergency.

The Navy unit will launch a torpedo boat (now stashed away in the Senate cloakroom) on the lake in front of the Lincoln Memorial and see that no enemy submarines penetrate to the Washington Monument.

These plans are contingent, of course, on Congress being in session. In case a filibuster is going on in the Senate when the balloon goes up, General Thurmond will be allowed to remain behind.

The Defense Department will probably deny these facts, but I have it on the highest authority that these plans have been drawn up.

Proof of it is that when I called the Defense Department and asked them what they were doing with so many high-ranking officers up on the Hill, a spokesman replied, "No comment."

TOP-SECRET PLANE

When President Johnson revealed at his news conference that the United States had developed a 2,000-mile-an-hour fighter-interceptor plane, the A-11, superior to any aircraft in the world today, he made headlines all over the world. This top-secret story had been kept under wraps for five years and it is believed that the only reason the President finally released the details to the press is that he did not have any other news to give that day.

But the plane the President failed to mention, which is far superior to the A-11 and is more radical than anything ever developed for the Air Force, is the PJ-306. Despite pleas from the Defense Department to keep the PJ-306 story a secret, I have decided to reveal the facts about it, as I believe that if the President can blow the story on a secret plane so can I.

I first heard about the PJ-306 when I visited Evreux Air Force Base in France in the spring of 1960. An officer who had too much to drink told me that the Air Force was working on a plane that could fly so low that nothing could hit it. Its maximum speed was 100 miles an hour with a good tail wind, or seven times less than the speed of sound.

He told me that the Air Force had been concerned for a long time over the Soviet development of supersonic aircraft. The Air Force, to keep up, demanded faster planes for itself until both sides had developed planes so fast they couldn't see each other.

At this stage, the Joint Chiefs of Staff decided they needed a new plane so slow that no fast Soviet fighter could shoot it down.

Everyone said it was impossible to develop such a fighter, and all the major airplane manufacturers were reluctant to work on it. So the Air Force turned the contract over to the Spad Aircraft Co.

The Spad designers and engineers worked on it for two years before coming up with the solution. They developed a bi-wing plane with one wing over the cockpit and one below it.

But then they ran into engine trouble. Every jet engine they put on the plane made it fall apart. When all looked lost, someone developed a radically new kind of engine, which they called a propeller engine. Although it sounds like science fiction, this engine has a large wooden stick on the nose, and when the engine is started up, the wooden stick turns and pulls air through the plane to give it buoyancy.

Air Force generals did not believe it was possible, but after the first trials at a secret air base they saw the plane take off and fly to an altitude of 500 feet in 20 minutes.

They were so impressed that they immediately ordered 500 of them and gave Spad the green light to go ahead.

Unfortunately, there were further delays. In order to have any value, the plane had to be armed. Spad placed a 50-caliber machine gun in the cockpit. But every time the pilot fired the gun he shot off his own propeller.

Finally the Massachusetts Institute of Technology was given the problem. They developed a method of synchronizing the machine gun with the turn of the prop.

The plane was ready to go into production.

The new plane has many innovations. The cockpit is open, so the pilot may jump out of his plane if hit. The landing gear is stationary, which gives the PJ-306 added slowness. So far nothing in the Air Force has been able to catch it, and in practice dogfights the PJ-306 has shot down 367 jet fighters.

Even Barry Goldwater has been reluctant to talk about this one.

ON THE BRINK OF PEACE

Is President Johnson bringing us to the brink of peace? Some people seem to think so and they're not very happy about it.

My good friend Jack Birch, who believes in war at any price, was very disturbed about President Johnson's references to nuclear disarmament in his State of the Union message to Congress. The President called for a reduction in nuclear stockpiling, a cutback in the production of enriched uranium,

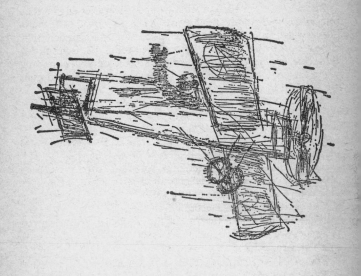

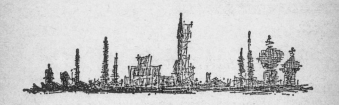

the shutting down of four plutonium piles, and the closing of many nonessential military bases.

As soon as Jack read the speech he called me on the phone.

"What does he think he's doing?" he said.

"I guess he's concerned about stockpiling too many nuclear weapons. I frankly think he's right."

"Oh, you think so," said Jack indignantly. "And what about overkill capacity? Have you thought of that?"

"What about our overkill capacity?"

"Our overkill capacity could be reduced to a new low. If we have the ability to kill everyone in the world 50 times under present conditions, and our stockpiles are lowered, we may only have the ability to kill them 30 times."

"But that's still pretty good," I said.

"Sure, you can say that. But how do we know what the overkill capacity of Russia is? Suppose their overkill capacity is 40 times. Where does that leave us?"

"I guess it means they could kill people 10 more times than we could."

"Exactly. Now remember, while we're reducing our overkill capacity, the world population is increasing at a frightful rate. And with every population explosion our overkill capacity is being reduced."

"But I don't think it will ever go below 30," I said, trying to placate him.

"Is that so? Well, I predict if things keep going the way they have been, we may be down to 15."

"That certainly isn't much of a margin," I said. "If you can only kill people 15 times, it hardly seems worth having a nuclear stockpile at all."

"I warned you what would happen if we had a test ban treaty," Jack said.

"But wait a minute, Jack. The United States has many non-nuclear weapons that we don't know anything about. It's quite possible that, if you added chemical warfare and the like, we could bring our overkill capacity over the basic minimums."

"We're not interested in minimums. We're interested in maximums. Whoever heard of anyone deterring someone with a minimum of destructive power?"

"Then what do you advocate?"

"What any patriotic person advocates. Resumption of tests,

building up of nuclear stockpiles, giving commanders in the field an option on whether they should use nuclear weapons or not, and increasing our overkill capacity to twice that of the Russians."

"That sounds reasonable," I said. "What can we do about President Johnson?"

"Impeach him."

"But you haven't even impeached Chief Justice Warren yet."

"Warren can wait. This is far more important. Johnson is sowing the seeds of disarmament and he'll have to pay for it."

"The only trouble is, Jack, that at the rate the Senate is working they may not get around to impeaching the President until we're down to 15."

"I knew you'd find something wrong with what I had to say. I'm sorry I called."

OUR DEFENSES ARE DOWN

The Defense Department has announced that it is closing down many military establishments in the United States in order to save money. Some of these bases, according to the Pentagon, have outlived their usefulness. When the news reached Capitol Hill, there were howls of indignation from our distinguished legislators.

To find out what all the screaming was about, I interviewed Congressman Michael O'Lobby from the State of Indignation.

"Is it true, sir, that you are very upset about the Defense Department's decision to close down military establishments in the United States?"

"You can bet your sweet life I am," O'Lobby replied. "I'm as economy-minded as the next Congressman, but when the Defense Department plays with the safety of our American citizens in the name of fiscal expediency, then I say there should be an investigation."

"Is there any particular military establishment that you are concerned about?"

"I certainly am. I am concerned about the closing of Fort Little Squaw at the mouth of the Ripahoodah River in my district. The closing of this establishment is one of the most dangerous military mistakes in our worldwide defense strategy."

"What function does Fort Little Squaw play in our defense?"

"I'm surprised you would ask that. Fort Little Squaw is the only fort west of the Mississippi to protect us from savage Indians."

"Indians? But there are no savage Indians in the United States anymore."

"Of course not. Not as long as Fort Little Squaw is in existence. But just close the fort and see what happens. Why, they'll come up the Ripahoodah River, overrun the plains, and before you know it, they'll threaten Grand Rapids, Detroit, and Cincinnati."

"I didn't realize they posed such a threat."

"Apparently no one in the Defense Department is aware of it, either. But the threat to America is not from without but from within, and believe me, son, you couldn't set yourself up for a better Communist conspiracy than by closing Fort Little Squaw."

"Communist conspiracy? I didn't know the Indians were tied up with a Communist conspiracy."

"Then why do they call themselves Redskins?"

"I never thought of that."

"Our national defense is based on a deterrent. The greatest deterrent we have against the Indians is the cavalry at Fort Little Squaw. If we close the fort, the Indians will swoop down on Chicago, scalping, massacring, pillaging, and setting fire to everything in sight."

"It sounds terrible," I said.

"You only have to watch television to see how terrible it could be. Fort Little Squaw is the last log cabin fort in this nation. How the Defense Department can say it has no value today is beyond the comprehension of anyone who loves his country."

"You make a very strong case for this particular military establishment," I said.

"I plan to make a stronger case at the next Armed Services Committee hearings. If the Defense Department doesn't see the military value of Fort Little Squaw, then I will not be able to see the value of any new nuclear submarines. What good is it to protect our front when we can be attacked from the rear? If we rely on nuclear weapons at the expense of the American cavalry, then our country is in greater danger than anyone thinks it is."

"I hope they change their minds."

"They'd better, or no white man will ever be able to sail safely up the Ripahoodah River again."

TO STUDY ROCKS

Last September, Representative Wright Patman said the CIA had been trifling with him, and so he revealed that the super-secret spy organization had been using a tax-exempt charitable foundation as a cover for its activities. The revelation cast a shadow on the role of all U. S. foundations and made people wonder how many are actually financed by the Central Intelligence Agency.

Not long after that a friend of mine applied to a foundation for a grant to study rock formations in the Catskills.

As he tells it, he walked into an office where a man who looked exactly like Gary Powers asked him to be seated. On his desk were parts of a U-2 that had been shot down.

"What can I do for you?" the man said.

"I'd like a grant to study rock formations in the Catskill Mountains."

"That's very interesting. Would you be willing to take a lie detector test?"

"I guess so," my friend replied. "But what for?"

"I'll ask the questions. Fill out this form, please."

My friend started to write. "There's no ink in the pen."

The man smiled. "Keep writing. We'll worry about that."

Then the man offered him a cigarette. As my friend accepted it, he distinctly heard a camera click.

"Now tell me about these rock formations."

"I don't know anything about them. That's why I want the grant."

"Have you ever thought about studying rock formations in the Urals?"

"No," said my friend, "the Russians would never let me in."

"Suppose you were parachuted in—at night?"

"If it's all the same to you I'd rather study rock formations in the Catskills."

The man said, "Our foundation is set up to help anyone who has an interest in science. How much do you think your expedition would cost?"

"Oh, about $900."

"We'll give you $15,000 if you'll go to the Himalayas."

"I don't want to go to India."

"I wasn't thinking of India. I was thinking more of Red China."

"Red China? If they caught me they'd shoot me."

"Not if your foundation provided you with a cyanide pill."

"Hey, what's going on? All I want to do is study rock formations in the Catskills."

"What do you know about rocks in Cuba?"

"Nothing."

"We could give you a $25,000 grant if you would like to study them."

"How would I get there?"

"Our foundation has a boat left over from some research we did at the Bay of Pigs. We'll also throw in a shortwave radio."

"To study rocks?" my friend said.

"You never can tell when you'll get lonely."

"If it's all the same to you, I'd just as soon not leave the country."

"Then I'm sorry, but I can't approve the grant. We have all the information we need on the Catskills. Of course, if you were thinking of going to Tibet . . ."

SOLVING THE OVERKILL PROBLEM

The problem of handling nuclear weapons was one of the issues of the 1964 campaign. Everyone was arguing about how many megatons of bombs and missiles could be delivered against the enemy in the next ten years.

The public was being asked to decide whether tactical nuclear weapons should be placed in the hands of generals in the field and whether we should give nuclear stockpiles to our allies.

I was very fortunate to interview Professor Max Kilaton, who had been working on the problem of nuclear weapons for some time. Professor Kilaton told me he made an independent study of the matter and came up with some startling results.

"The most important thing I discovered," he said, "was that while the Russian and American nuclear bombs are large enough, the targets for most of them are too small. We must build bigger targets to fit our bombs."

"I don't understand."

"Well, you see you have small bombs now that are five or ten times more powerful than the ones dropped on Hiroshima and Nagasaki, and you have larger bombs and missiles a hundred times more powerful. But you have no cities whose growth has been comparable to that of the bombs. Therefore, if you dropped a large bomb on a major city, there would be a great deal of waste in fallout, heat and power. In order to compensate for this, I am advocating the immediate building of larger targets."

"You mean make the cities bigger?"

"Exactly," Prof. Kilaton replied. "We must start an immediate building program to enlarge our cities so the radius of our most powerful nuclear weapons will fall within them."

"Would the Russians go along with this?"

"They would have to. They could not let our targets get bigger than theirs. It would be too much of a blow to their prestige."

"How could we make our targets worthy of the nuclear weapons which have been stockpiled?"

"We must build up urban centers between our large industrial cities and more or less connect them. The cities would have to be large enough to take a hit of the most powerful nuclear weapon that the Russians have. They in turn would have to enlarge their cities to accommodate our nuclear bombs."

"But what would this accomplish?"

"It would solve the major problem of nuclear weapons, which is overkill. If your targets are large enough for your bombs, you would eliminate the problem of overkill. That is, you would kill exactly the number of people the bomb was designed to kill. As it stands now, most of the larger nuclear weapons can destroy only one-twentieth of their potential. This is sheer waste and certainly works a hardship on the economies of the nuclear powers."

"What about tactical nuclear weapons?"

"You have no problem there. A good tactical nuclear weapon can destroy an average city with a bare minimum of overkill, perhaps 2.5 percent. Most targets are suitable as they now stand for tactical nuclear weapons. But the big danger is that if you use tactical weapons you could escalate your war to the point where you would have to use your big stuff and then your targets would be wholly inadequate."

"One more question, Professor. Do you think we should give nuclear weapons to NATO allies?"

"I certainly do. If Greece and Turkey both had nuclear weapons at their disposal, I believe the problem of Cyprus would have been solved weeks ago."

III. F. I. N. K.
☆☆☆☆☆☆☆☆☆☆☆☆☆☆☆☆☆☆☆

NO LEG TO STAND ON

The topless bathing suit has not been very successful. The reason for it is that men wouldn't go along with it. They threatened their women, "If you wear a topless bathing suit, I ain't going swimming with you."

So the fashion designers got sore and they said, "We'll fix 'em."

How did they fix us? They decided to cover women's legs, with wool, flowers and rhinestone stockings. If we are to believe the fashion writers, the slim, clean leg of yesteryear is being replaced by what looks to be the fifth leg of a dining room table.

I can speak with authority because I happen to be a leg man. The first thing I look at when a girl walks by is her legs. The Buchwalds have always been leg men. They started out, of course, as ankle men in the days when women weren't allowed to show their legs, but as skirts got shorter we started to specialize in limbs, and I remember my daddy once saying to me when I was six years old, "I envy you, son. At your height, you can see legs better than I can."

As I grew up I became a great admirer of the female limb. But I was a purist. All I asked was a nice, shapely calf in a sheer silk or nylon stocking supported by an attractive ankle and a high heel. I wanted no frills to detract from the view. Women could do what they wanted with the rest of their clothes, but I demanded their legs remain clean, neat and, if possible, straight.

I did most of my memorable leg watching at sidewalk cafe tables in Paris.

78

I could sit for hours on end, either with French or American friends, looking at limbs as they went by. Sometimes the waiter would join me and we would discuss the merits of a French leg as opposed to an American leg. It was hard work but it had its rewards.

Then a little over two years ago the shades of the stockings started to get darker. I wasn't worried at first, as I thought it probably had to do with smog or something. But pretty soon the realization dawned on me that women were starting to wear black stockings.

I became very upset. The black stockings, if they were sheer, were not unattractive, and in some cases had a certain sex appeal. But my main fear was that the stocking people were about to spring something on the public that might change the entire course of leg-watching.

When I expressed my apprehensions to my French friends, they laughed at me. "Legs are too important to women," they assured me. "They would never do anything to detract from them."

I wrote my daddy and he wrote back, "I'm scared, too, son. I think we're in for a bad time."

It took two years before the prediction came true, Sure enough, this year the new stockings were put on the market. Harlequins, diamond patterns, birds and even porpoises were woven into the patterns. Every color under the rainbow was introduced.

Despite the fact that the stockings make women look like Italian coffee tables, they have been selling well. The joys of leg-watching are disappearing right under our eyes. Last Sunday I took my son for a walk, just as my daddy had taken me, and after it was over my son said, "What's so great about legs?" I didn't know what to reply.

IT'S BETTER TO GIVE

I have this aide who works for me and I must say he's becoming quite a problem.

One day I said, "Bobby, take these photographs down to the post office and mail them for me."

"Yes, sir," he said, "but before I go, I would like to give you and Mrs. Buchwald this beautiful hi-fi stereo for your lovely house."

"That's very nice of you, Bobby, but it isn't Christmas."

"I know, sir, but working for you means so much to me I don't know how to repay you."

"Well, thank you very much. I'm sure Mrs. Buchwald will be thrilled."

A few days later I said, "Bobby, go out and get me a cup of coffee and a doughnut."

He took the quarter, but when he returned he was struggling with a large crate which was almost bigger than he was.

"Sir, I know all you wanted was coffee and a doughnut, but I would like you to have this electric barbecue pit as a token of my esteem," he groaned breathlessly.

"Bobby," I said gently, "I appreciate the gesture, but are you sure you can afford something like this on your $40-a-week salary?"

"Certainly, sir. You're the finest person I ever worked for and you'll hurt my feelings if you don't take it."

A week went by and one day Bobby came into the office and said he was finished filing all my old columns, and asked if I would take a drive with him.

I was very annoyed, but he was persistent. Bobby drove me out to my house and, lo, right in the backyard was a new swimming pool.

Bobby smiled.

"What's going on?" I demanded.

"Sir, the last person I worked for was mean and cruel and always yelled at me. You've never raised your voice and I appreciate it. The only way I can demonstrate how much this means to me is to present you with this Olympic-size heated swimming pool."

"Thank you so much, Bobby. I'm terribly moved. Now you'd bettter get back to the office and fill the water cooler."

For a month Bobby worked very hard and I didn't see too much of him, though occasionally I found a gift from him on my desk. One time it was 50 shares of AT&T. Another time it was a gift certificate from Tiffany's for Mrs. Buchwald. A third time it was a go-cart for the children. But I thought nothing of it.

After all, I had exchanged gifts with Bobby for years. Once I gave him a ball-point pen, another time I presented him with two tickets to a Washington Senators game, and only a few weeks ago I had bought him a key chain with a likeness of the Capitol in silver plate dangling from a link.

But I did get worried last week. I had just come back from being examined for an insurance policy when I found Bobby waiting excitedly at the door of the office.

He said, "I know I'm just an office boy around here, but I've learned a great deal from you and I have to show you how much I appreciate all you've done for me."

"You don't have to do that, Bobby."

"There are some bosses you hate," he said, "and others you'd die for. You're in the second category. And to show you how I feel, I'd like you to have this."

He handed me a sheet of paper.

"What it is?" I asked him.

"It's the deed to Disneyland. You now own it."

"Bobby, you shouldn't have."

"Sir," he said with tears in his eyes, "the pleasure is all mine."

EXTREMISM AT HOME

There has been a great deal of confusion over the words "extremism" and "moderation" and everyone is trying to clarify what they mean. Senator Goldwater wrote a "Dear Dick" letter to former Vice-President Richard Nixon in which he explained how he used these words. Little did I realize that I would have to clarify my use of them in the same week. I had a fight with my wife, and since we weren't talking, she sent me a letter asking me to clear up several things I said in the argument.

Her letter read:

DEAR SIR:

Since our meeting three days ago, I have received several inquiries from my mother and friends concerning your use of the words "extremism" and "moderation." The charge has been made that in using these words you were in effect approving recklessness and unlawful activity in achieving a sound and happy home. I have assured all of those who have raised this question with me that you would be the first to reject the use of any illegal or improper methods to achieve the great goals to which all of our family is striving.

I believe, however, that it would be most helpful if you would clear the air once and for all in this regard, and I would appreciate it if you would send me any further comments you wish to make respecting the intended meaning of these two words.

Sincerely yours,
ANN BUCHWALD

DEAR MRS. BUCHWALD,

Your letter was most welcome. Misunderstandings must not be permitted to stand in the way of unity of the family. Much has been said about my use of the words "extremism" and "moderation" in our discussion of the other evening. But when they are seen in their correct context, I am sure you will agree that I used the words correctly.

When I called you an extremist the other night, I was only referring to the way you spend money on the house. I did not mean to insult the political convictions of your mother, who happened to be there at the time. I used the word only after you showed me the bill for the $600 dining-room table, which came, I might remind you again, without chairs.

Your mother's retort, that extremism in the pursuit of affluence was no vice, was uncalled for and clouded the argument. My plea for moderation in spending was interpreted by both you and your mother to mean that I had a no-win policy when it came to furnishing the home.

All I was demanding was some reasonable solution to a very difficult economic situation.

I admit that I said that I would have to resort to some extreme measures if the spending spree did not stop, but this was no reason for your mother to call me a member of the John Birch Society.

While it is true that I did say that anyone who spends more than her husband makes is leading him down the extreme path to Communism, I did not call either one of you Communists by name as you are said to have told your sister Joan.

I know that my cause is just, and I hope that this letter clears up the matter as far as both you and your mother are concerned. If you use "extremism" to mean wholehearted devotion to the family budget and "moderation" to mean halfhearted devotion to the household economy, then I'm sure my words could not be interpreted in any other way. Looking forward to seeing you at the summit conference.

Sincerely yours,
ART BUCHWALD

PRAYING IN SCHOOL

The Congressional hearings concerning the "prayer in school" issue had been going on for several weeks last May and were thought to continue right into the summer.

Hundreds of witnesses had demanded to testify in front of Congressman Celler's committee and there had been a great deal of passion at the hearings.

It seemed to me that a compromise should have been found between the forces who "want to put God back in school" and those who were defending the First Amendment of the Constitution which guarantees the separation of church and state.

I've studied the question not only from a Constitutional point of view but from a practical one and these were my findings.

I found that school children do not want to pray all the time. They pray only when the spirit moves them.

In discussing prayer with children, one student told me, "I only pray in school so I won't get hell at home."

Another student said, "I always ask God to help me when I haven't done my homework."

"Does it work?" I asked him.

"It worked once. He made my regular teacher sick and the substitute didn't ask for our papers."

A teacher told me that she discovered over the years that the children who prayed the most in school were those who did the least studying at home.

"I find those students who watch television the most are the same ones who are always calling for help from the Deity the next morning."

A young girl said, "I think kids should be allowed to pray before a test."

Another young lady said, "There are no atheists when report cards come out."

Many students do not think much about God until their school is playing the big game of the year against an archrival. Then, while the ball is on the two-yard line and the other team has four downs to score in, all eyes go up to the heavens imploring the Almighty to "hold that line."

In a certain community, a test was given to see if prayer had any effect on the students. Half the class used prayer and

the other half used another brand. It was discovered that the
half that used prayer had far less cavities and were happier
than those who didn't pray.

But the main point I was trying to make is that pro-
prayer people want prayers every morning while the anti-
prayer people want no prayers at all in school. No one has
come up with "Selective Praying." Why not let children pray
only before tests, when report cards are due, and when promotion time comes around? This is when they need it the
most.

They're going to do it anyway, and it's better to have them
pray openly in class than sneak into the locker room or into
the washroom for a quick prayer where no one will see them.

BUT DON'T GET INVOLVED

I've seen examples of ordinary citizens who have witnessed
crimes and done nothing about them. Their excuse has been
they didn't want to get involved.

If we reach the ultimate of the non-involvement syndrome,
we may have something like this:

A dark street, a man walks home from work. Out of the
shadows pops a holdup man. "Your money or your life."

"Please, I don't want to become involved."

"What do you mean, you don't want to become involved?
I'm holding you up."

Just then a man goes by. "Hello, Harry, what are you doing
out so late?"

"I'm being held up by this fellow."

"I didn't see anything," the second man says and dashes off.

"Hand over the money," the gunman says.

"You're making a mistake. Suppose they catch you? Then
I'll have to go to court and testify. You know how much time
that takes? Maybe your case won't be called for months."

Just as the holdup man lifts his pistol, a window opens and
the man's wife shouts, "Harry, why don't you come upstairs?"

"I can't. There's a fellow down here holding me up."

"We don't want any trouble. Tell him to go away."

"I can't. He wants my money. Maybe you should call the
police."

"I don't want to get involved, Harry," his wife says.

Another window opens. "What's going on down there?"

KEEPING US INFORMED

The airlines have a new public relations gimmick. Just as you get bedded down in your seat for a cross-country flight and start to snooze, a voice comes over the loudspeaker: "This is your captain speaking. We are flying at an altitude of 35,000 feet and on our left is the city of Palm Springs."

You peer out the window and all you see is a mass of clouds.

"Of course you can't see it so good at the moment," he says, "but it's a wonderful town."

You doze off again to be suddenly awakened by the friendly voice. "We have just passed into Arizona," the pilot says.

You start applauding until the other passengers stare you down.

All is well until 15 minutes later when the voice is back again. "We will soon pass over the Grand Canyon, which will appear off our right wing. The weather should be clear."

Several passengers take out their cameras and one of them asks if I wouldn't mind moving so he could get a picture. I move over to the left side of the plane.

"Before arriving over the Grand Canyon," the voice says again, "I would suggest you look out the left side of the plane at the glorious mountain range."

The passengers with their cameras rush back to the left side windows and I'm asked to move again.

"Now coming up ahead is the Grand Canyon."

The camera-toting passengers reverse themselves and they're back on the right side.

Just as everyone is in position, the friendly voice says, "We may be hitting a little turbulence. I would suggest everyone fasten their seat belts."

The passengers reverse themselves again and return to their seats.

"Would you mind taking a picture for me?" one of the passengers asks.

I hold the camera against the window and press the button. "Did you get it?"

"How the hell do I know?" I say honestly.

Word reaches the pilot that we will soon be passing over Oklahoma City, and he just can't keep it to himself.

When the pilot isn't informing us about geography, he's

telling us what the weather is like in Chicago. He also fills us in on his latest engine change, explains why the motors will sound different. Then he tells us he's going up 5,000 feet to avoid a rainstorm, and 25 minutes later he informs us they have hurricane warnings over Florida but, since we're not going there, we have nothing to worry about.

For 45 minutes I hear nothing and I start to worry. I call over the stewardess and ask her, "Is there anything wrong with the pilot?"

Before she can go up front to check, he's back again.

"We've just passed over Lima, Ohio," he announces triumphantly.

I breathe a sigh of relief.

I guess it's a good idea to keep everyone informed on how the pilots are flying the plane, but I can't help wishing for the good old days when they were busy up front with the stewardesses and left the passengers alone.

DIVORCE—TELEVISION STYLE

Hello, Mom, is my wife there? . . . What do you mean she won't talk to me? She's being ridiculous . . . I know she's sore at me, but it's been almost a week now. How long can she stay mad? . . . Nothing happened! Nothing at all . . . You only heard her version . . . Saturday, that's when it all started.

I'll admit I agreed to rake the leaves, but that was before I realized the Pitt-Syracuse game was on TV . . . What's wrong with watching a football game on TV? . . . I know I also listened to the Notre Dame-Navy game on the radio, but it was the Game of the Week . . . I did too talk to her Saturday afternoon. I distinctly remember asking why she hadn't put any beer on ice.

She said I wouldn't come to dinner? That's not exactly true. I had to watch the big race at Aqueduct and then there was *Wide World of Sports* and I said I'd come in after that, but it was just my luck there was a hockey game on next. You don't see much hockey on television anymore . . . I told her I'd eat my dinner in the TV room and do you know what she said? She said, "I'm not running a hotel. You can get your own dinner!" Now, is that a nice thing to say to somebody who's watching a hockey game? . . .

Aw, Ma, you know how she exaggerates. The wrestling

matches ended at eleven o'clock. She knew I liked wrestling when I married her. I came to bed right after *College Scoreboard*.

Sunday? I guess I did say something about raking leaves on Sunday, but first I had to read about the Notre Dame-Navy game and then the big race at Aqueduct and then the hockey game, and before I knew it it was time for the Redskin-Eagles kickoff on TV. That's not true. I did let her into the TV room. I only told her to get out after she asked me what color drapes I wanted in the bedroom just as Charley Taylor was running for a touchdown . . .

Did she tell you that? . . . Did she also tell you that she wouldn't give me any lunch unless I brought in the dirty dishes from Saturday night? Now I ask you what kind of wife is that? . . . I didn't yell at her . . . I may have raised my voice when it was fourth down, touchdown to go, and she told me to take all the summer clothes up to the attic, but I did not use violent language . . . She gets everything wrong . . . I didn't watch the Detroit-Rams game after that. It was Buffalo against Houston. And it was a very important game. How many doubleheaders do you get on television? . . . Okay, so I forgot we invited the Winstons over for drinks. I wasn't rude to them. I showed them where the bar was and said I'd see them in a couple of hours. How did I know they were going to go home before *Great Moments from Pro Football* was over?

Listen, Mom, you talk to her. I'm getting tired of eating TV dinners and there isn't a clean dish left in the house.

And tell her I love her and miss her and the children very much . . . What did she say? She said she'd come back? Great, wonderful. When does she want me to pick her up? . . . Saturday. Gee, I can't Saturday. Illinois is playing Michigan and it could mean an invitation to the Rose Bowl.

WHITHER THE COCKTAIL PARTY?

Will the Johnson Administration go down in history as the one which ended the cocktail party as we know it? There has been a tremendous amount of agitation in Washington over President Johnson's announcement that he expected his staff to put in long hours of work and avoid cocktail parties as much as possible. Probably no edict in recent history will have such an effect on the nation's capital.

The Washington cocktail party is as important to democratic government as the right to vote. Our nation could not have survived without it.

The first known cocktail party to have played a part in American history took place in Boston the day after the Boston Tea Party. A great party was scheduled that day at the home of Mr. and Mrs. John Adams. Mrs. Adams planned to serve tea and cookies, but when all the tea was dumped into Boston harbor, she had no choice but to serve whiskey and gin.

"Hey," one of the American colonists said, "this stuff tastes better than tea."

As the party continued and the colonists kept filling their teacups, the conversation became more anti-British and pretty soon the Bostonians started talking about insurrection.

The colonists decided at the party to take on King George III, something they would never have done if they were sober.

The next morning every one woke up with a hangover, but it was too late. Word had gotten out about what they planned to do, and the rest of the colonies were inspired to take up the cause.

When Washington was established as the nation's capital, the cocktail was moved with it.

In 1803 some French land promoters gave a cocktail party on what is now the site of the Internal Revenue Service. They were pushing some worthless swamps in a place called Louisiana. Thomas Jefferson showed up at the party and after about six drinks the hosts talked him into buying the land for $15 million. Jefferson didn't have the cash with him, so he gave the promoters a check.

The next morning, when he realized what he had done, he tried to stop the check, but it was, fortunately for the United States, too late. The promoters had already picked up the money and left for Paris.

During President Monroe's tenure of office, the Distillers' Institute, a whiskey manufacturers' lobbying organization, decided to introduce a new drink named after the President. They wanted to call it the Monroe Doctrine (two parts Southern Comfort, one part sour mash). Mrs. Monroe served the drink at a cocktail party, and it was such a big success that

President Monroe decided to name his whole foreign policy after it.

One of the great vices of the Republic, according to historians, was drunkenness. Agitation for drinking reforms started in the early 1850s and a group of Washingtonians decided the only way to make people cut down on liquor was to free the slaves who served it.

Without servants no one could have a cocktail party. Thus the abolition movement was started, not as an anti-slavery measure, but as an anti-liquor movement. The South decided it wasn't worth remaining in the Union if they couldn't have free servants for their cocktail parties, so they seceded from the Union.

The man who did the most for the Washington cocktail party was Ulysses Grant, whose eight-year Administration consisted of one party after another. It was during President Grant's terms of office that one of the most famous slogans in American advertising was devised: "As long as you're up, get me a Grant's."

And so it went through history. Each Administration rose or fell on the basis of the Washington cocktail party. Foreign policy, domestic politics, newspaper exclusives, military promotions, defense contracts, have all been made at cocktail parties. It's hard to believe that President Johnson would, in the interest of getting his people to work late in their offices, make us all go back to drinking tea.

WHY HUSBANDS ARE COWARDS

I went to see *Hello, Dolly*, the new smash musical with Carol Channing which had just wound up its Washington run before going on to Broadway.

Although we had nothing but praise for the cast, the music, the costumes and the staging, I can't say as much for the audience, particularly the lady who was seated behind me. She not only did her utmost to ruin the show for me, but she almost broke up my marriage.

The lady turned out to be one of those compulsive talkers who always seem to find out ahead of time what seat I've purchased and then buy theirs directly behind me.

This lady loved the show. Every time Miss Channing sang a song, she commented on it to her husband. "Isn't she wonderful?" "Isn't she darling?" "What a lovely costume." "That's a fine song." And so on. Before the first act was over I was trying to climb the wall, which is very difficult in any theatre.

"She's driving me crazy," I said to my wife.

"Don't you do anything silly," my wife warned me.

"I could kill her," I said. "That's not silly."

"Behave yourself," she said threateningly.

As soon as the first act curtain fell and we went out into the lobby, I said to my wife, "I'm going to tell her off."

"You can't," she said.

"Why not?"

"You'll embarrass me."

"How will I embarrass you if I tell her to shut up? Will she think any less of you if I ask her to keep quiet?"

"You'll make a spectacle of yourself," she said.

"That woman is spoiling the show for every one around us. If I say something, everyone will be grateful. I could be a hero."

"If you say anything, you'll spoil the show for me."

"And if I don't say anything, I'll ruin it for myself. Why are wives always afraid their husbands are going to embarrass them? If you saw that woman in a department store at a sale, you wouldn't hesitate to knock her over to get to the counter. Why are you defending her in a theatre?"

"She probably can't help herself," my wife said angrily.

"Neither can I. You would think her husband would tell her to shut up."

"Would you tell me to shut up if I talked during the show?"

"I certainly would," I said.

"That shows what kind of manners you have."

"What has that got to do with the woman behind us?"

"I wouldn't be surprised that if you said something to her she'd slap you in the face."

The bell rang and we all returned to our seats.

As soon as Miss Channing came out, the woman started up again.

I turned around and said, "Would you please shut up so the rest of us can hear the show?"

The woman turned white, but not as white as my wife.

"George, that man insulted me," the woman said to her husband.

"Now you're in for it," my wife whispered.

The husband turned out to be about six foot one and

weighed 200 pounds. After the show I started up the aisle and he followed me. As soon as I got to the door he spun me around and stuck out his hand. "Thanks a lot, mister. I didn't have the nerve to tell her myself."

BEYOND THE CALL OF DUTY

The Christmas Shoppers' Honor List has been published and medals of heroism were passed out to this year's recipients in a moving ceremony in the Rose Garden of the Department of Commerce. Families of the recipients gathered there to see their men decorated with the Christmas Shoppers' Medal of Honor, given to those who have risen beyond the call of duty when it came to purchasing gifts for the holiday season.

The first person to be cited was Phil Stern, a horticulturist from Nyack, N. Y. Stern decided to take his four children to F. A. O. Schwartz, the toy store, on a Saturday afternoon two weeks before Christmas. Despite warnings that it was a suicide mission, Stern attacked the Fifth Avenue side of the store, but was repulsed by overwhelming enemy forces.

Refusing to be defeated, he then struck the 58th Street entrance where he managed to gain ground and fight his way through to the second floor where he established a bridgehead in front of the electric train display. Though suffering from shock, he managed to rally his patrol and keep them together.

Under heavy fire, he made a reconnaissance mission of the second floor before he was forced to retreat to the first floor. Stern returned to headquarters with valuable information that made it possible for his wife to attack on the following Tuesday.

His actions were in the highest tradition of the Shoppers' Corps, and gave inspiration to other fathers who refused to leave Nyack during the holiday season.

Emmett Dedmon of Chicago was cited as follows: "Mr. Dedmon heard there was a sale on lingerie at Marshall Field's, and without hesitation volunteered to take on the mission. He rushed into the department store and was immediately flung to the ground by a hundred angry women shoppers. Though his leg was broken, Dedmon crawled to the counter and captured a nightgown, which was torn out of his hand.

"Suddenly someone threw down a pair of lounging pajamas on the floor, which Mr. Dedmon covered with his body, thus saving the lives of hundreds of customers in the building. He managed to crawl toward the door with four purchases and, when asked to surrender, he said 'Nuts!' "

Henry Rogers of Los Angeles, California, was the third recipient of the CSMH. "Ordered by his wife to go to a discount record house to buy several Beatles records, Rogers arrived just as school vacation had started. In hand-to-hand combat with several screaming teen-agers, he managed to wrest three records from them before he was thrown against a hi-fi set and knocked out. When he recovered consciousness on the floor, he remained absolutely still and the teen-agers left him for dead.

"A few hours later he made his escape. When interviewed later, all Mr. Rogers could mumble was, 'Yeah, yeah, yeah.' "

The last medal went to Robert Yoakum of Lakeville, Connecticut. Yoakum came to New York to go Christmas shopping with his children. He also promised to take them to see the Christmas show at Radio City Music Hall.

When Yoakum saw the line around the Music Hall, he said: "I'm not going to stand in line."

So he ran up to the front of the theatre and tried to push his way in.

His medal was awarded posthumously to his widow, who said, as she tearfully accepted it from Secretary of Commerce Hodges:

"Bob was always like that."

EXTREMISM IN PURSUIT OF UNICEF

The John Birch Society has become one of the best merchandising outfits in America. A few weeks before last Christmas the head of the John Birch Society in Monterey got terribly upset because a department store and two banks in his town were selling UNICEF Christmas cards, the proceeds of which went for children around the world. He threatened the store and the banks with picketing if they didn't stop selling the cards.

The publicity from the affair was so great that the Christmas card sale, which had been lagging, suddenly picked up steam and in many places UNICEF cards sold out.

Many fund-raising organizations have been studying the Monterey incident with envy. The tuberculosis Christmas Seal people have asked the John Birch Society if they would picket stores which sold Christmas Seals. They have even offered to provide signs and police protection, but so far the John Birchers have refused to help.

Other organizations that have begged the John Birch Society to attack them are the Salvation Army, the March of Dimes, and the Heart Fund. The argument is that it is unfair to single out UNICEF and make them the beneficiary of all the Birch attacks.

"If the John Birch Society really cared about children," a fund-raising official said, "they would picket all children's charities so the money could be divided equally."

Another fund-raiser said, "I think the John Birch Society is defeating its purpose when it threatens to picket one organization. They should devote their energies to picketing the United Community Fund, which raises money for many different kinds of charity. It should be a community effort."

It was pointed out that the reason the John Birch Society picked on UNICEF was because some of the funds went to Communist nations.

"We'll give some of our funds to Communist nations, too, if that's what it takes," the official replied.

A Christmas Seal official said, "UNICEF benefits by two holidays, Christmas and Halloween. The John Birchers have raised so much hell about kids collecting money for UNICEF on Halloween that the UNICEF take has been doubled. I think the only fair thing is to let the John Birch Society picket UNICEF on Halloween and Christmas Seals in December."

The real problem seems to be that although the John Birch Society says it's growing in numbers it still doesn't have enough members to picket every charity that needs them.

In the case of Monterey, there were only enough pickets to take care of one department store and two banks. Many places that were selling UNICEF Christmas cards weren't even threatened.

The John Birch Society is not to blame.

They're doing the best they can, but they just can't fulfill all the requests they receive for picketing charitable institutions.

It was suggested that token Birch picket lines could be

thrown around hospitals and orphanages for the benefit of
the press and these organizations could profit from the photographs. But until the Birch Society increases its membership
the only ones who stand to gain are the UNICEF people.
It's no wonder all the other charitable organizations are sore.

ANYONE FOR SUBTITLES?

The Robert F. Kennedys are a close-knit family, and Ethel
Kennedy is a strong-willed person and thereby hangs a tale.

A few weeks ago the Kennedys decided to take their children and a few friends to a film in Washington, D. C. It was
the first outing for Mr. Kennedy since his election, and he
was looking forward to it.

They chose what they thought to be a cowboy picture
titled *That Man from Rio,* but when they got into the theatre
they discovered it was a French comedy with English subtitles.

Mrs. Kennedy was very upset, particularly since several
of the children couldn't read.

She told Mr. Kennedy she would get their money back
and would go to another movie. She went outside to the box
office and explained to the cashier she didn't know the picture
was a foreign one and asked for her $14.50 back.

The cashier said it was against the policy of the theatre to
refund any tickets and anyone should have known it was a
foreign picture just by the cast.

Mrs. Kennedy retorted that it was up to the theatre to
advertise they were showing a film with subtitles and she
demanded to see the manager.

The manager finally arrived and Mrs. Kennedy explained
the situation again.

The manager was no more sympathetic than the cashier.
He said the policy of the theatre chain was no refunds. Mrs.
Kennedy said she had several children with her who couldn't
read subtitles and she had been bilked.

The manager offered to let her take the ones who couldn't
read across the street to see *Rio Concha,* an American film.
Mrs. Kennedy said she refused to split her family.

As an afterthought she said, "I know Pierre Salinger, and
he may become the head of the Motion Picture Producers
Association, and I'm going to see the first thing he does is

make a ruling that your theatre must indicate on the outside when it is showing a foreign film."

Mrs. Kennedy was so adamant that the manager finally said, "All right, lady, I'll mail you the $14.50. What's your name?"

"Mrs. Robert F. Kennedy."

The manager gulped. "Any relation to the Senator?"

"His wife."

"You can get your money back now."

Mrs. Kennedy went back to the box office, but the cashier told her she would have to wait in line. She said she wasn't moving until she got her $14.50.

The cashier realized she meant business and said, "Give me the stubs."

Mrs. Kennedy could find only 12 stubs. She needed 14.

The cashier called the manager, and he said, "Give her anything."

It took 40 minutes, but Mrs. Kennedy swept into the theatre triumphantly with the money in her hand. She told Mr. Kennedy they could leave now. Mr. Kennedy said, "I don't want to leave. This is one of the funniest pictures I've ever seen."

All the children shouted, "We don't want to leave. We're going to stay until it's over!"

With tears in her eyes, the pregnant Mrs. Kennedy returned the $14.50 to the box office.

The happy side of the story is that Mrs. Kennedy is still talking to Mr. Kennedy—but just barely.

THE TEEN-AGE MATRIARCHY

Teen-age-ologists, the experts who spend their time studying the habits and mores of teen-agers, have just come up with some more frightening information.

It appears the female of the species is taking over more and more as the head of the tribe, and teen-age-ism is fast developing into a matriarchy.

A recent study by Lester Rand, of the Youth Research Institute of New York, reveals that the female teen-ager is slowly getting control of the purse strings of the teen-age male. Rand's survey revealed that teen-age boys were turning over their allowances and earnings to their "steady" girls. Teen-age girls seem to have convinced their boy friends they can manage their money better and make it go farther.

"I have discovered," Mr. Rand said, "that some teen-agers even have joint bank accounts."

Mr. Rand also discovered that teen-age girls were putting their boy friends on budgets and deciding what they should buy in the way of clothes as well as luxuries.

"In many cases," Mr. Rand said, "the girls badger their boy friends into demanding larger allowances and wage increases. Girls also seem to hound unemployed lads into getting jobs so they can have more spending money."

The survey revealed that male taste in clothes, haircuts and even automobiles was being dictated by the female teen-ager.

"I don't know why, perhaps it's parental influence," Mr. Rand said.

The extent of the influence can be sadly dramatized by what one youth told Rand in Boston. "My girl wants me to be asleep by eleven and, since she lives next door, she checks my bedroom light to see if it is off."

The teen-age girl also plays an important role in deciding the education of her boy friend. One boy revealed he wanted to go to Tufts, but his girl wanted him to go to Boston College, her father's school, so that is where he is going.

Mr. Rand also discovered that teen-age girls actually select careers for their boy friends. One youth, who was on his way to becoming an accountant, changed over to law when his steady informed him she would never marry an accountant. Unfortunately, in this case, after he started law school, she got engaged to someone else.

The report also revealed that teen-age young ladies make the decisions on what films their boy friends will see, what records they will hear, and what television programs they will watch.

The so-called "teen-age market," which is said to be worth billions of dollars, is controlled almost entirely by the female, just as the grown-up market is controlled by her mother.

What does this all mean? Mr. Rand says that teen-age boys are much more lonely and insecure than teen-age girls. They submit to all the indignities because they can't resist female flattery, and they're suckers for anyone who listens to their troubles.

It's almost impossible for a teen-age boy to resist a girl who pretends she has his best interests at heart.

The tragedy is that, at the very moment teen-age boys are fighting to break away from parental control, they are meekly handing their hard-won victories over to their girl friends.

Mr. Rand concludes, "The American husband of the future gives every indication of becoming completely housebroken. Most of the spadework is being done now."

(Attention, teen-agers. When writing to protest this scurrilous article, please send a stamped, self-addressed envelope.)

THE AFFAIR

One of the problems of being married and having young children is that much of the romance goes out of people's lives. A friend of mine has solved the problem. Every week he has an "affair" with his wife.

What he does is he kisses his wife good-bye in the morning and goes off to work. About noon he calls her up and whispers, "This is George. Is your husband home?"

His wife replies, "No, the oaf has gone off to the office."

"I've got to see you this afternoon," the husband says.

"I can't. I've got to be home when the children come from school."

"Get one of the neighbors to take care of them. Tell them it's an emergency and you have to go into town."

"Do I dare?"

"Please, darling, we don't have much time together."

"I'm frightened."

"I love you."

"I'll come. Where shall we meet?"

"Somewhere where no one will recognize us. I'll pick you up on the corner of F and 14th Street, at three o'clock."

The wife arranges for the neighbors to take care of the children and gets dressed up in her prettiest suit. She then drives into town, parks two blocks away and waits on the corner.

Her husband pulls up. She glances around fast and then hops in.

"I think I was seen, darling," she says nervously.

"Relax," the husband says comfortably.

"Where are we going?" she asks.

"There's a motel just across the bridge. We'll check in there."

"But we have no luggage," she protests.

"I'll check in. You stay in the car and then we'll drive to the room."

After they get into the room she laughs, "I didn't even bring a toothbrush."

"I thought about you all week," he says, kissing her.

"So did I," she replies. "I waited for this moment. I thought it would never come."

"I wanted to call you, but I was afraid he would answer the phone."

"He wouldn't stop watching television to answer the phone. Does your wife know about us?"

"She's too busy taking care of the kids to know about anything. I told my secretary if she called to tell her I was out at a conference."

"How long can we go on like this?"

"Let's just be grateful for what we've got."

"If we'd only met each other before."

"I feel that way, too."

At six o'clock they check out of the motel, and my friend drops his wife off at F and 14th. "Until next week, my darling," he says as he kisses her.

"It will seem like a year," she says tearfully.

She hops out of the car without turning back.

An hour later her husband arrives home. "Anything happen today?" he asks casually, as he pecks her on the cheek.

"The same dull routine. Anything happen with you?"

"No, just another crummy day." He yawns. They both smile inwardly and sit down to dinner.

F. I. N. K.

Several years ago I happened to write about a mysterious organization called FINK. Similar in many ways to SMERSH and UNCLE, though much more sophisticated and ruthless, FINK has only one purpose and that is to prevent someone from getting any sleep.

At the time I revealed that several FINK agents were following me around Europe. As soon as I checked into a hotel, one of them got the room above me, ripped up the carpet and started dropping his shoes on the floor. Another FINK agent checked into the room next to me and coughed all night long, while two other agents, pretending to be man and wife, started a fight in the room on the other side at three o'clock in the morning.

I thought when I moved back to the United States I had gotten out of the clutches of FINK, but it turns out I was wrong. FINK is everywhere.

On a recent lecture trip to the West Coast I was fast asleep on the plane when a FINK hostess woke me up and asked me whether I would like a cocktail.

I thought it might have been just a coincidence, but when I got to Salt Lake City, I realized FINK was onto me. Somehow they had gotten a copy of my itinerary, had bought the land across the street from my hotel, and just as I arrived they started putting up a new building.

Moving on to San Francisco I discovered that four FINK agents disguised as gas company employees had been set to dig up the street with pneumatic drills, just below my hotel room.

I checked out in the middle of the night and went to a motel on the outskirts of town, thinking I had outwitted them. But I was a fool. FINK had placed a sports car driver right outside my window who had orders to race his engine all night long.

Weary and frightened, I went to Los Angeles and sought refuge in a very fancy Beverly Hills hotel. But FINK had arranged with the managers to renovate all the rooms on my floor as I was dozing off.

I finally got out of town and went to Houston and registered under a false name at a soundproof airport hotel. I dropped on the bed and immediately went to sleep. But not for long. A FINK chambermaid came into the room and woke me up.

"I'm sorry," she said, "I didn't know there was anybody in the room."

"What does FINK want from me?" I shouted. "I'll give you money, I'll give you state secrets, I'll give you anything, if you'll just let me sleep."

She denied she worked for FINK and stuck to her story that her waking me up was an accident.

Seven sleepless nights later I got back to Washington and the safety of my own home.

After kissing the children and eating a late supper, I headed straight for bed. But at one o'clock in the morning I felt a gentle tugging on my arm. As I woke up, my wife said, "I think I hear somebody downstairs."

Suddenly it dawned on me—the most frightening thing of all. FINK had somehow gotten to my wife and she was now working for *them*. I knew I was doomed.

IV. FATHERS FOR MORAL AMERICA

☆☆☆☆☆☆☆☆☆☆☆☆☆☆☆☆☆☆☆☆☆☆☆☆☆

FATHERS FOR MORAL AMERICA

There has been a great deal written about an organization called Mothers for Moral America. The Mothers organization had planned to put a "moral decay" film on television which showed the worst aspect of American life, from topless bathing suits to pornographic literature. At the last minute the film was withdrawn.

Another organization has just been started, called Fathers for Moral America, which is also concerned with moral decay in the United States.

When I visited its headquarters the other day, a spokesman for the organization told me, "The mothers have done so much to point out the decadent aspects of the United States that we felt the fathers should help out, too."

"What do you do?"

"We have a screening room in the back where we show dirty movies every two hours. We want to alert the fathers of America to the terrible degeneration that is going on in the United States. The response has been heartwarming. Ever since we started the screenings, there hasn't been an empty seat in the house."

"What has been the reaction?"

"The majority of them leave shocked that things like this could be happening in this country, and many come back a second time because they can't believe it."

"What else do you do?"

"At luncheon every day we hold a fashion show at which we display the latest topless bathing suits which have been put on the market.

"We want the fathers to know just exactly how far this nation has slipped, and, believe me, once they see the models in the topless bathing suits, they never forget it."

"It must be terrible to see," I said.

"I've seen men so horrified they have refused to eat their lunch."

"What else have you done to show the deterioration in American morals?"

"We have a reading room over there where we display the latest collection of salacious books and magazines. Any indignant father can go in there and see the type of literature that is being peddled around the country."

"The room seems very crowded," I said.

"It is one of the most popular exhibits. Many fathers have requested permission to take the books home, but we're afraid we'd have trouble getting them back. Some of the stuff would make your hair stand on end."

I walked into the reading room and noticed many of the fathers' hair standing up straight.

My guide took me out into the hall. "This is our souvenir counter where we sell photographs and slides of the different burlesque queens. We've been urging fathers to show them at home and at smokers to illustrate what we're up against. We also sell twist records and French postcards as part of our educational program."

"It seems to be doing well," I commented.

"You would be surprised how many alarmed fathers have offered to help in this great crusade."

My guide took me upstairs. "This is our telephone center. We have father volunteers who tell anyone who calls in what to watch for on television or at their local theatres, and what books to read. This is one of the best ways of getting our story over to the American people."

"I'm emotionally impressed with your great work," I said. "When does the next movie go on?"

THE REAL DANGER

The Supreme Court is having a terrible time defining obscenity. Everyone is agreed they're against it, but no one really knows what it is. In reversing a conviction on the French film *The*

Lovers six opinions were filed on the case with six judges all expressing their own views on the subject.

The irony of it all is that since *The Lovers* was first shown in the U. S. several years ago, there have been far wilder pictures shown in America without any complaints.

Many people are worried about obscenity, but I'm worried about something which I consider far more dangerous to America—and that is the flood of clean movies that are now being released on the market.

No matter where you look these days there is a clean movie playing in some theatre in your neighborhood. Of course these movies are advertised as dirty movies and you wouldn't know from the posters outside that they are clean, but once you get inside you find yourself treated to the worst kind of wholesomeness imaginable. Scene after scene is devoted to children and pets and sports and domestic tranquillity—all aimed not to advance the plot, but only inserted for its shock value.

The makers of these pictures, led by the most notorious clean producer of them all, Walt Disney, defend these films as works of art. But then they add, "We wouldn't make them if the public didn't want to see them."

One director said, "If other companies would stop making clean movies, so would I. But this is a very competitive business."

Another director said he was forced into the clean pictures by the foreign films. "I tried to make obscene films but I lost my shirt, so I decided to go for the clean movie. My feeling is that if people don't want to see this type of movie they don't have to."

"But aren't you concerned about the effect clean movies will have on our young?"

"Kids know more about wholesomeness than we do," he said defensively. "We don't aim these pictures at kids, but we can't stop them from seeing them."

Attempts to set up some kind of code to eliminate wholesome scenes from films have failed.

A spokesman for the industry said, "The problem is no one can seem to agree on a national standard for cleanliness. Until the Supreme Court decides this question, the motion picture industry can do nothing to stop the sudden rash of unsullied productions now being produced in Hollywood."

An American civil liberties lawyer told me, "Trying to eliminate clean movies would be an abridgment of the First Amendment. If we are going to put up with dirty pictures, then we'll have to put up with clean ones as well."

Until the experts can decide what constitutes a really wholesome movie it will be up to each individual to decide for himself whether he wants his family to see a clean movie or not.

Do not be misled by the advertising. Many films which promise obscenity are really wholesome films. The best way to eliminate this type of picture is to protest to the local manager, and tell him if he ever shows a clean film again you're going to take your family business somewhere else.

THE TOPLESS WOMAN

News reaches us from the heart of the New York fashion industry that the topless bathing suit and the transparent evening gown are now being sold to top stores around the country.

For years designers have been working on a breakthrough in swimming and evening apparel without any visible success. But 1964 will go down as the year the bottom fell out of the top, and historians in centuries to come may mark it as the date when women returned to the cave.

Nobody had bothered yet to get the reaction of men to this most interesting and disquieting bit of news, so I took two photographs—one of the topless bathing suit and one of the transparent evening gown—out into the hot Washington streets to ask how the male sex felt about the whole thing.

First I showed them the photographs and then I asked them what they thought.

The first man I spoke to said, "M-m-my my g-g-g-osh, wh-wh-wh-ere did y-y-ou buy th-th-those d-d-dirty pictures?"

"They're not dirty pictures," I said. "They're fashion photos of the latest bathing suits and evening gowns. Would you want your wife to wear a bathing suit like this?"

"S-s-ure, except sh-sh-she can't sw-sw-swim."

The second man I showed the bathing suit to was horrified. "My God," he cried, "they've covered up the navel."

"Yes sir," I said, "they had to in order to do away with the top."

"How prudish can you get?" he said in disgust and walked away.

The third man I spoke to studied the transparent evening gown for a while and then said, "I don't care what they do, as

long as they tell us what to do when they wear one of those things."

"What do you mean by that?"

"What are our instructions? How are we supposed to behave when a girl comes out in one of those? I mean are we supposed to stare or ignore her or ask her to dance?"

"I guess each man will have to decide for himself."

"I think I'm against it," he said.

"Why?"

"It will make my shirt wilt."

The fourth man I talked to said, "I think I seen that girl in *Playboy* magazine."

"I doubt it," I said. "This is a high-fashion model and she only works for dress designers."

"Well, there's something familiar about her."

"What do you think of the idea of the swimming suit?"

"It came out too late," he said.

"Why too late?"

"It should have been put on the market for Mother's Day."

The fifth man looked at the photograph for about ten minutes. "If you want my honest opinion, I think this evening dress is a shocking disgrace."

"Why do you say that?"

"The bow should be in the back of the skirt. Any designer knows that."

Two teen-agers were peering over his shoulder and one said, "And they're always rapping us for juvenile delinquency."

The last man I talked to said, "I think it's a good idea."

"Why?"

"It will give the missionaries in America something to do."

ANOTHER VALACHI?

I don't know about the rest of the country, but my family was very much impressed by the Valachi hearings that were going on in October of 1963. One evening, at 1 A.M. to be exact, as I was about to go to sleep, my wife said:

"I have something to tell you."

"What is it?"

"Joel stole some money today."

Joel is ten years old. Stealing runs in the family, and so I didn't get too excited about it.

"How much did he steal?"

"Five cents," she replied.

"You better call the McClellan Committee," I said, punching the pillow several times.

"Don't make a joke of it. It isn't the money that concerns me. It's the fact that he lied about it. When I asked him where the five cents was, he said he lost it. I found out later he spent it on candy."

"A regular Cosa Nostra," I said. "Can't we hold hearings on it in the morning?"

"Well, you may want your son to grow up and be a gangster or a racketeer, but I don't. You're taking this entirely too lightly."

"All kids steal at ten years old," I said, trying to use logic, which is always a mistake at midnight. "And when they steal, they lie about it. What kind of a thief would he be if he confessed just because you asked him to?"

"Did you ever steal at ten years old?"

"Did I steal? I stole everything, and none of this penny-ante stuff, either. If it wasn't worth a quarter, we weren't interested."

"You certainly are setting a fine example. If you want to know the truth, I think Joel has criminal instincts."

"All ten-year-old boys have criminal instincts," I said. "Stealing and lying are part of growing up."

"But if he wanted five cents, why didn't he ask for it?"

"Because that's not any fun. Stealing is fun. You can't imagine how delicious candy tastes when it's been bought with stolen money."

"I don't like your attitude at all. I've been watching those hearings on television and I don't mind telling you they scare me."

I thought the discussion had ended and I was just dozing off when she said, "Maybe we should give him riding lessons?"

"What for?" I said, trying to stifle a yawn.

"So he'd have an interest in things. You don't do anything with him. No wonder he's turning into a criminal."

"What do you want me to do with him?"

"Take him fishing. Play football with him. Do what other fathers do with their sons."

"I don't like fishing. He doesn't enjoy playing football with me and I don't think I should change my way of life because he stole five cents."

"Probably Valachi's father said the same thing about his son."

"I don't know if that is so or not. But I have a theory as to why Valachi went bad."

"What's that?"

"The reason Valachi turned into a criminal is because his mother would never let his father go to sleep at night."

DREAM INTERVIEW WITH MISS KEELER

I had a dream interview with Miss Christine Keeler the other evening. Actually I planned to have a dream interview with the Prime Minister, but when Miss Keeler came into view I decided to talk to her instead. I could always speak to the Prime Minister in a dream at another time.

Miss Keeler was simply dressed in a smart gray suit and when I spoke to her she was just getting out of a Rolls-Royce.

"I say, Miss Keeler, I wonder if I could have a few words with you?"

"Please hurry," she replied, "I have to go to a ban-the-bomb meeting in a few minutes."

"Miss Keeler, rumor has it that you had indiscriminate affairs with several men, including John Profumo, former Minister of Defense, and a Soviet naval attaché."

"The rumors are outrageous. I've only known both men intimately."

"Is it true, Miss Keeler, that you used to go swimming in Lord Astor's pool at Cliveden with no clothes on?"

"Yes, I was trying to make the British women's Olympic team for 1964, and Lord Astor said I could practice in his pool."

"But while you were practicing one night, is it not true that you met Mr. Profumo at the pool?"

"Yes, I did. Since he was a member of the Cabinet, I was hoping he would use his influence to get me on the team."

"So your interest in Mr. Profumo had to do with your swimming career?"

"Exactly. Mr. Profumo was very impressed with my swimming and he felt if I practiced very hard I would be able to go to Japan in 1964."

"Did you believe him?"

"I don't know, but when the scandal broke several people

offered to send me to Japan in 1963. They must have had faith in my swimming to want to send me a year ahead of time."

"Miss Keeler, it has been reported you were a very good friend of Dr. Stephen Ward's. What exactly was your relationship with him?"

"He was my swimming coach. He felt I had talent and he offered to introduce me to other men who could help me make the team."

"Did he?"

"Yes. Through him I met several people of importance who felt that if anyone should make the Olympic team it was I. Some even offered to give me money to buy me a bathing suit. But I refused as I was afraid it would hurt my amateur standing."

"Miss Keeler, it has also been rumored that you were very friendly with a Russian naval attaché. Is this true?"

"Yes. I knew the Russians were expected to have a very good swimming team at the Olympics and I was hoping to learn from him some of their secrets."

"Did Captain Ivanov ask you to get any information from Mr. Profumo?"

"On one occasion he asked me to ask Mr. Profumo what the West German Olympic team hoped to accomplish at Tokyo."

"Did you help Dr. Ward find other girls to coach for the Olympic team?"

"Yes. He was interested in other swimmers, and every time he saw a girl that he thought could make the team he asked me to introduce her to him."

"Did they all express an interest in wanting to make the team?"

"Stephen was determined to make good swimmers out of all of them. Although some didn't qualify, he did get most of the girls in deep water before he was through."

"But now that there is a scandal, do you think you will still make the Olympic team?"

"I'm not sure. Lord Astor won't let me use his pool anymore, so I don't know where I'll practice. And the men that offered to help me make the team now claim they never heard of me. If nothing happens, I'll probably join the Aquacade. I've been offered 10,000 pounds a week to swim across the pool twice nightly at the 1965 World's Fair in New York. The only trouble is this would make a professional of me and I'm not sure I'm ready for it yet."

HOPE FOR UNWED FATHERS

With all the bad news going on throughout the world last July there was one ray of hope emanating from, of all places, England. A welfare council in Essex announced that it had set up an agency to help unmarried fathers.

Roy Demery, who was appointed by the Moral Welfare Council of Essex, was quoted as saying, "Unmarried fathers must be helped, not neglected and looked down on.

"The fact that a girl is having his baby obviously weighs heavily on many a man, especially if he is not in the position to marry her. . . . Often he is bullied into wedding her by angry parents. This should not happen if the couple don't love each other."

I hope that the Essex experiment is a success and a similar program will soon be adopted in this country. The problems of unwed fathers have been ignored by everyone in the United States, while all the attention has been concentrated on the unwed mother. And yet for every unwed mother there is an unwed father somewhere—alone, friendless and needing sympathy.

There are an estimated 3,000 homes in the U. S. where an unwed mother can apply for help, but there is not one place where an unwed father can seek consolation.

Having spent four years in the U. S. Marines, three years at the University of Southern California and fourteen years in Paris, I have always been concerned with the plight of the unmarried father.

Friends have come to me in the darkest hours of the night and tearfully confessed that they had fathered a baby. All I could tell them was, "Forget it."

But this, unfortunately, wasn't enough. Many of them were filled with guilt and despair. Some wanted to run away, but they had no place to run to. A few were being pursued by angry fathers and brothers with shotguns and hid out with me until the danger was over. And then there were desperate ones who had lost all reason and wound up marrying the girl. Had there been a welfare agency to help them, none of it would have happened.

Now perhaps all this will be changed. If the Essex experiment is successful unwed fathers will have a new lease on life.

The way I see it is that when an unwed father finds out he's going to have a baby he goes to the agency and registers with them. A social worker will explain to him that there is no shame in being an unmarried father and he will be introduced to other unwed fathers who are in a similar boat. In this way he'll realize he is not alone.

Two months before the baby is born the unwed father will be sent away to a resort area where he can relax and enjoy himself without fear of being recognized or scorned by unfriendly neighbors and relatives.

When the baby is born the unwed father will be notified and he can return to his community with no one being the wiser. Perhaps he could be paid a small stipend from the agency until he gets on his feet again.

In time society may develop a different outlook toward unmarried fathers. But until they do I think this is the best solution to a problem that for too many years has been swept under the rug.

MARRIAGE BY COMPUTER

Dr. Eric Riss, a sociologist, insists marriages made through computers are more successful than those made in heaven.

Through in-depth personality tests and swift calculations of an 0-82 IBM electronic computer, Dr. Riss is said to have mated 730 couples with only two divorces. He has been pairing people for the past eight years.

"Most people fall in love and then they try to find out if they are compatible," he said. Dr. Riss's method is much more scientific. He makes a personality profile which he transfers to a punch card which is fed into an IBM sorter, which finds a card representing an applicant of the opposite sex whose likes and dislikes, educational background, temperament, ambition and goals shape up suitably. Then a match is made.

I'm not too concerned with the 730 successful marriages arranged by Dr. Riss as much as I am by those two divorces. Where did the computer go wrong? Let's look in on one of the two couples.

Mrs. Jones comes into the living room. "What happened to us, George? We seem to be drifting away from each other."

"I don't know," George says. "Something must have happened to our personality profile analysis."

"Is there another woman, George?"

"Of course not. Somebody just punched a wrong hole in my IBM card. It could have happened to anyone."

"But we do have the same temperament," Mrs. Jones says.

"That's true," George says. "And our ambitions are similar. We both want me to be rich."

"We both love to play golf and to watch *The Defenders* on television," Mrs. Jones says.

"I have a B.A. from college and you have a B.A. from college, so it couldn't be our educational differences," George says.

"We both read the same books and enjoy the same music."

"When we travel we always like to visit the same places and I don't think we've ever had a quarrel about our vacation."

"No, we haven't," Mrs. Jones says. "You seem to eat everything I cook for you."

"I do and I like it. Our taste in food is very similar."

"Even our dislikes are the same. You don't like to dance and neither do I. You hate to go out to cocktail parties as much as I do. We both dislike our in-laws."

"As far as the house goes," George says, "I have no quarrel with your choice in decoration."

"And I've always been interested in your work," Mrs. Jones says.

"We seem to be perfectly matched," George says.

"Then what could it be?" Mrs. Jones says.

"We've thought of everything," George says.

"Not everything. Let me ask you something, George. Do you love me?"

"No," George replies. "Do you love me?"

"Of course not," Mrs. Jones replies.

"Then that's it," George says. "Why didn't I think of it before?"

Mrs. Jones breaks down and cries. "It wasn't your fault, George. The IBM machine can't think of everything."

FATHERS ANONYMOUS

One of the results of sending American troops all over the world is the rise in the birth rate of little half-Americans fathered by the American GIs. No one wishes to take any responsibility for these children, just as very few people will admit they exist.

Miss Pearl Buck, one of our greatest living authors, has been concerned about the problem for some time, and has started a foundation to take care of some of these children, particularly in Korea, where our troops have contributed so generously to the population explosion.

Miss Buck was in Washington whipping up some interest for her foundation.

"I have discovered my cause is not a popular one," she told me. "The American mother won't believe her son would have an affair. The veterans' organizations are shocked that I would even raise the question, and the American military are completely defensive about it. 'How could our boys do such a thing,' the military say, 'when they were playing volleyball all the time?'

"I have tried to point out that the only other possible way for the children to arrive would be by stork, but unfortunately there are no storks in the Far East."

Miss Buck said she has a solution to the problem that wouldn't embarrass any one. She has started Fathers Anonymous, which will make it possible for a father of a half-American to contribute some money without anyone knowing about it.

"I am sure," she said, "that there are quite a few men in this country who are conscience-stricken and would like to do something about it, if it wouldn't get them in trouble. Fathers Anonymous is the perfect answer.

"If any GI or ex-GI can remember a wonderful occasion during his service years that could have resulted in a baby's being born nine months later, then he is eligible to join Fathers Anonymous.

"All I am asking is that in grateful memory of that evening he send a cash contribution to my foundation. The beauty of my organization is that there will be no questions asked, no names required, and no follow-up on the contribution. The money sent can be considered conscience money. I am certain there are many veterans who would like to ease the burden of their guilt if they could. As Sophie Tucker said recently, 'Okay, everyone had a wonderful time. Now let's clean up the mess.' "

I asked Miss Buck why she felt the American GI had fathered so many Oriental babies.

"I think it was a language problem. A GI couldn't speak the

young lady's language and the lady couldn't speak the GI's language, so they had nothing much else to do."

"How much conscience money do you think some one should send in?"

"Perhaps enlisted men could send in $5—junior officers $10 and senior officers $20. If they send in cash to me at Perkasie, Pennsylvania, without a return address, there is no possible way of their being found out. I can't think of a nicer way of making it up to the girls they left behind."

"Miss Buck," I said, "how would some one be sure he should join Fathers Anonymous?"

"I can think of one test," she replied. "If the person's hands are shaking while he reads your article, you can be sure he has a reason to be a member of the club."

SUBTITLES FOR OLD BOOKS

There was a time when the only way you could get a pornographic book was to smuggle it in from Paris. But in recent years the paperback book industry in the United States has been outdoing anything you could bring in from Paris. I feel everyone has a right to make a dollar under our free enterprise system and if people want to buy pornographic literature that is their business. What I object to is the publishers making nonpornographic books pornographic by putting half-naked women on the covers of good books and printing descriptions of the contents which give an entirely different idea of the plot.

If the trend continues, here is how our paperback publishers will soon describe some books familiar to all of us:

Snow White and the Seven Dwarfs—The story of a ravishing blond virgin who was held captive by seven deformed men, all with different lusts.

Cinderella—A beautiful passionate woman bares her naked foot to the man she loves while her stepmother and stepsisters plot to cheat her out of the one memorable night in her life.

Alice in Wonderland—A young girl's search for happiness in a weird depraved world of animal desires. Can she ever return to a normal happy life after falling so far?

Huckleberry Finn—A wild youth runs away from his home to help a Negro slave escape from the ravishing Miss Watson.

Little Women—Four teen-agers, wise beyond their years, are caught up in the throbbing tumult of the Civil War. Read what happens to them when a rich old gentleman and his greedy grandson take rooms as boarders in a house without men.

Tom Brown's Schooldays—For the first time we look beyond the locked doors of an English boarding school to reveal the truth about a life that no one talks about and only a few will whisper.

Treasure Island—The crew of a ship bent on rape and plunder land on an island inhabited by sex-crazed cannibals. An innocent boy finds the secret of growing up.

Little Red Riding Hood—A girl goes to visit her grandmother only to discover a wolf in her bed. Read what happens when the girl refuses to get into bed with the wolf.

Tom Sawyer—A gang of subteen-age hoodlums paint the town white, and commit mayhem and murder to satisfy their desires.

Heidi—A young lady caught up in the wild life of Switzerland fights for love.

Babar the Elephant—Life in the raw.

And so it goes. As for the covers, I'll have to leave that up to the publishers. I hate to think what the paperback artists will do with *Wind in the Willows*.

V. BLUE EYES AND GREEN TEETH

☆☆☆☆☆☆☆☆☆☆☆☆☆☆☆☆☆☆☆☆☆☆☆

IS HEAVEN SEGREGATED?

One of the better shows in Washington during the summer of 1963 was being held by the Senate Commerce Committee on the public accommodations law, part of the late President Kennedy's civil rights package. The law would make it compulsory to serve and accommodate someone regardless of race, creed or color.

Two Southern governors were helping out poor Senator Strom Thurmond, who seemed to be the only one on the committee fighting against the law. Both Governors Ross Barnett, of Mississippi, and George C. Wallace, of Alabama, claimed the Negro demonstrations were Communist-inspired. They also claimed "their" Negroes were happier than Northern Negroes because "their" Negroes knew where they stood.

Governor Ross Barnett said he once asked a Negro whether he would rather be white or black and the Negro is said to have replied "he'd rather be black, particularly on Saturday night in Jackson, Mississippi."

Governor Wallace was asked by Senator Hart of Michigan: "What do you think heaven will be like? Do you think it will be segregated?"

The Governor replied, "I don't think any one of us knows what heaven will be like. . . . God made us all. He made you and me white, he made others black. He segregated us."

The Governor had a good point and it gets one to thinking, maybe there are two heavens, one for whites and one for blacks.

This is probably God's way of keeping everyone happy.

But as far as the segregationist is concerned, I'm not too sure the white heaven would be such a heaven without Negroes.

First of all, in heaven there are an awful lot of white sheets to wash. Secondly, in order to really have a nice heaven, you would have to keep it immaculately clean. This is work the Southerners depend on the Negro for. Presumably even in heaven there are crops to harvest and meals to be cooked and children to be taken care of and doors to open and cars to be parked and lawns to be mowed and shoes to be shined and garbage to be removed, and without Negroes the segregationists would have to do it themselves. If the segregationists have to do all the tasks the Negro people have been doing on earth, you couldn't call it very much of a heaven.

Also a segregationist's idea of heaven is a place where, no matter how bad off he is, there is somebody worse off in the neighborhood. That's why the white Southerner claims he loves the Negro. It gives him such a heavenly feeling to know that, no matter how black things are, they could be worse if he were black.

As far as Governor Wallace and Governor Barnett and Senator Strom Thurmond were concerned, I doubt if they could have gotten elected to any office without the racial question, and I hope for their sakes there is only one heaven so they could continue their fight for segregation in the Great Beyond.

But on the other hand, if there are two heavens in the hereafter, one for whites and one for blacks, I believe, if I was a segregationist, I'd rather go to hell.

THE WAYWARD BUS

I walked into the office of a New York newspaper the other day and found a Negro friend of mine completely downcast.

"What's the matter?" I asked him.

"I just moved to a nice section of the Bronx," he said, "into a lovely house on a nice street with grass and flowers and trees. The neighbors gave me no trouble—as a matter of fact, they were very nice to me. The kids were happy as could be. It cost me $3,000 a year more, but I didn't care. It was worth it."

"What happened?" I asked.

"Now they want to bus my kids to school in Harlem."

"That doesn't sound right."

"They figured my kids should be with underprivileged kids

so they'll know what it's like. But I told them my kids know what it's like in an underprivileged school and we'd like to try an overprivileged school for a while."

"What did they say?"

"They said I should have stayed in Harlem if I wanted my kids to go to a good school. I can't expect them to go to a good school if I'm going to live in a good neighborhood. That wouldn't make sense."

"They have a point, you know," I said. "If everyone who lived in a good neighborhood sent their kids to a good school, whom would you send to the bad schools?"

"But I don't know why I have to live in a bad neighborhood to send my kids to a good school."

"Because the schools in a bad neighborhood are bad, and you wouldn't want to send them to a bad school, would you?"

"That's why I moved in the first place," he said.

"Well, you should have thought about it before you moved. Just because you live in a good neighborhood is no reason why you should send your kids to a good school."

"It's not as simple as that. I have a friend who lives in a bad neighborhood but, because of the busing, the authorities decided to make it a good school. They fixed it all up and brought in some first-rate teachers. Then they bused his kids to a good neighborhood which had a lousy school. He complained he wanted his kids to go to the good school in the bad neighborhood, but they told him his kids had to be bused to the lousy school in the good neighborhood, so the kids from the good neighborhood would have a good school to go to in the lousy neighborhood."

"Well," I said, "if that's true, why wouldn't your kids be able to go to a good school in a lousy neighborhood?"

"Because the school they want to send my kids to is a lousy school in a lousy neighborhood. Besides, how are my kids going to meet any kids from the good neighborhood if they go to the lousy school?"

"Maybe on the bus?" I suggested.

"I don't think so. I believe there is only one solution. I think I'll move back to Harlem and send the kids to private school."

THE BIG DISAPPOINTMENT

The civil rights bill has been a landmark in American history. Unfortunately, although it provides that there should be no discrimination in restaurants and hotels based on color, no provision was put in the bill to guarantee the quality of the food.

This was probably a mistake.

A while back I interviewed a Negro from Birmingham, Alabama, who had been served in one of the leading hotels there for the first time and he told me he was disappointed.

"All my life," he said, "I had been under the impression that the food in this hotel was great. Why else wouldn't they let us eat there? So as soon as the civil rights bill was passed, I said to my wife, 'Mother, let's go down to the hotel and have a fine gourmet dinner.'

"She was delighted because she never gets out much.

"Well, we went to the hotel and asked for the dining room. I thought it would be something special since they kept us out of it so long, but it turned out to be an ordinary hotel dining room with bad lighting, rickety chairs, and very cheap ashtrays.

"They didn't give us much trouble when we asked for a table, although the manager, out of curiosity, inquired who recommended the restaurant to us. I told him the 88th Congress of the United States and he seemed satisfied."

"How did you find the service?" I asked him.

"Very indifferent. I was particularly disappointed by the dry martinis. We like our martinis very dry. When the drinks arrived, we were distressed to discover a four-to-one ratio between gin and vermouth. I should think it wouldn't be difficult to make a good martini in Birmingham."

"What about the food?"

"I'm quite a lamb fancier, so I ordered the roast lamb. My wife had the escalope de veau milanaise. We both ordered Caesar salad. I know you won't believe this, but they left the croutons out of the salad."

"And what about the lamb?"

"A little too well done for my taste, and while I hate to be critical, I found them too sparing with the garlic. My biggest disappointment, though, came when I asked to see the wine card. I was informed they didn't have a wine card and the waiter offered us a red burgundy which I knew was too young, quite inferior, and would never show its promise. I expressed dissatisfaction and the waiter said it wasn't his fault. Up until the civil rights bill was passed, the restaurant served only white wine.

"This put a pall on the dinner."

"How was dessert?"

"The cheeses weren't very interesting and the choice of desserts was appalling. I had to use all my influence to have them make me a baked Alaska. It was a disaster."

"What did you do?"

"I told the manager that, if he wanted our people's patronage in the future, he would have to improve the quality of the food."

"What did he say?"

"He thanked me for my criticisms and said that from now on they would try harder."

BLUE EYES AND GREEN TEETH

Governor George C. Wallace is a reasonable man. When he makes a point for segregation, he never attacks the Negro head on. He always resorts to using another type of illustration. He will say when arguing against the civil rights bill, "You may want to sell your house to someone with blue eyes and green teeth and that's all right. I don't object. But you should not be forced to do it. A man's home is his castle."

Recently I had my house up for sale in Washington and what Governor Wallace said took on meaning for me. Several people looked at the house but no one seemed to want to buy it. Then a man arrived with his wife. He was very nicely dressed, and seemed very polite. The thing that struck me about him was his blue eyes. I was just about to sell him the house when he smiled and I noticed he had green teeth!

"I'm sorry," I said as gently as I could, "but I can't sell you the house."

"Is it because I have green teeth?" he asked.

"Well, if you want me to be honest, yes, it is. I promised my neighbors I wouldn't sell my house to anyone who had blue eyes and green teeth. If you had green eyes and blue teeth, or brown eyes and yellow teeth, I could do it. But you have to understand, my home is my castle."

The man turned to my wife sadly. "You are the fourth per-

son who has turned me down. It's not my fault that I have
green teeth. I've tried every toothpaste on the market. I've
consulted every dental specialist in the country. All they figure
is that there is something in my genes. Please, won't you sell
your house to me?"

"We couldn't if we wanted to," my wife said. "It isn't just
because you have blue eyes and green teeth. Your wife has
green teeth also."

His wife spoke up. "Of course I do. Who else would marry a
blue-eyed green-toothed girl except another person with the
same coloring? I thought I was going to be an old maid until I
met Harold."

I said, "And I suppose your children have blue eyes and
green teeth also?"

Harold said they did.

"You can see the spot I'm in, can't you?" I said to him. "This
neighborhood is made up of brown-eyed and white-toothed
children. What would their parents say if their kids had to go to
school with children with blue eyes and green teeth? If God
wanted your children and mine to play together, he would have
made their eyes and teeth the same color."

"But I want to give my kids a chance," Harold said. "How
can a kid with blue eyes and green teeth improve himself if he
doesn't have an opportunity to live in a decent neighborhood,
go to a decent school, and have the benefits that kids with white
teeth have?"

"If it were up to me alone, I'd probably sell you the house,"
I said. "But if I did, the next thing you know is that everyone
with green teeth would start moving in. Real estate values
would tumble. Blue-eyed people would start marrying gray-
eyed people and before you know it you'd have a mongreliza-
tion of the races."

Harold said, "We don't want to marry people with gray eyes
and white teeth. All we want is a decent place to live. I make
a good living posing for television toothpaste commercials. I'm
the one who uses Brand X. But I want my kids to do something better in life. Can't you understand?"

"I understand perfectly," I said. "But nobody else does."

THREE CHEERS FOR DISCRIMINATION

Last spring, actor Peter Lawford and his wife, Pat, sister of the
late President Kennedy, were turned down in their efforts to

buy a New York apartment. It seems that all prospective tenants for this particular apartment house are screened by a Board of Tenants. One member of the board, Francis Masters, turned down the application, although the other four members of the board said they had no objection to the Lawfords' moving in.

Mr. Masters' excuse for blackballing the couple and their four children was that Mr. Lawford was an actor and Mrs. Lawford was a Democrat.

Since the story appeared, Mr. Masters has received a great deal of criticism for his stand. I think it's time somebody came to his defense.

Every one knows what kind of people actors are. They stay up late at night, they have parties, they get their names in the gossip columns, and people are always asking for their autographs. Very few of them go to church and they have wild orgies around their swimming pools, and if you pick up any movie fan magazine you'll realize they are driven, tormented people. No God-fearing family would want them living in the same apartment house.

Mr. Masters had every right to object to Mr. Lawford's moving into his building. You let one actor in and pretty soon other actors want to get in and real estate values go down and the neighborhood goes to hell. Just look what happened to Beverly Hills and Bel-Air when they allowed actors to live there.

But I believe that Mr. Masters might have made an exception in Mr. Lawford's case if it weren't for the second problem, and that was the fact that Mrs. Lawford was a Democrat. No apartment house in New York could stand having a family composed of an actor and a Democrat at the same time.

There is no need to go over the type of tenants Democrats make. They never throw out their garbage, their kids are always yelling and screaming, they get in fights with Republican children, they hold meetings in their apartments for Medicare and civil rights, and you never know what kind of visitors you're liable to meet in the elevator. I know of one apartment house that had Democrats living there, and one day a Republican tenant saw Adlai Stevenson, Arthur Schlesinger and Walter Reuther—all going in at the same time.

The trouble with Democrats, as everyone knows, is that they keep to themselves. Even if you offer to be friends with them, they reject you. Their interests are different and they don't want to mix with you any more than you want to mix with them. It's one thing to have integration of the races, but it's another to have integration of people who belong to a different political party.

One of the reasons there is no provision in the Fair Housing Law guaranteeing rights for people of Democratic convictions is that Democrats can't assimilate with people of other backgrounds.

In every case where it has been tried, the crime rate in the neighborhood has gone up and the apartment houses have gone to ruin.

Mr. Masters knows this better than anybody. Instead of criticizing him, people should say to themselves, "Would you want your children to play with children who have an actor for a father and a mother who is a Democrat?"

THE STALL-IN

Not only has the stall-in caper of militant civil rights demonstrators caused ill-feeling at the New York World's Fair, but the repercussions have spread to the rest of the country.

Anyone who runs out of gas now on a major highway is an immediate suspect.

Two days after the World's Fair publicity on stall-ins a friend of mine ran out of gas on a highway outside of Washington, and this is what happened. He flagged down another car. When it stopped, he said to the driver:

"I'm sorry to bother you, but I just ran out of gas."

"Oh, you're one of those guys," the driver said menacingly.

"No, you don't understand. My wife forgot to fill up the gas tank yesterday."

"She's one, too, huh? I ought to punch you right in the nose."

"Please, I don't want to get into a fight," my friend said. "I just want some gas."

"All you guys are for non-violence," the driver snarled.

Several cars stopped to see what was going on.

"This guy says he's run out of gas," the driver said.

"Let's lynch him," another driver said.

My friend started to get nervous as the crowd enlarged and cars started to honk their horns.

"If someone would just help me push it over on the grass, I'd be most grateful," my friend said.

"Sure," said someone in the crowd, "and then you'll push it out on the highway again."

"I won't," my friend promised. "I'll go buy some gas."

"You should have thought of that before you started the stall-in."

"Has anyone got a cattle prod?" a voice yelled.

"I don't need a cattle prod," my friend said. "I just need some gas."

"What did you do, drive from Brooklyn to start trouble down here?"

"No, I live around here."

"Oh, so you're a local agitator."

"I'm not an agitator," my friend said.

From the crowd he could hear people saying to one another, "What happened?"

"Some Commie says he ran out of gas."

"Throw him in the jug."

"What happened?"

"That guy waving his arms says he's going to turn on all the tap water in Washington to protest civil rights."

"What happened?"

"Fellow threw himself in front of a car because they won't hire Negro bus drivers."

Finally a policeman came along and my friend explained that he was out of gas.

"They got an injunction against guys like you," the cop said.

"Look, just call a tow car and take the car away," my friend said.

"You're not going to get off that easy," the cop said. "Okay," he said to the crowd, "break it up. Everybody gets a fair trial —even a stall-in."

They towed my friend's car away and finally let him go. When he got home he could barely speak to his wife.

"Where have you been?" she wanted to know.

"You forgot to fill the tank yesterday," he said bitterly, "and I've just been made an honorary Black Muslim."

MODERATE BIAS GOES A LONG WAY

It has not been released yet, and the Surgeon General's office will deny it, but there is a top-secret report in the files proving that prejudice causes cancer.

The statistics show it also causes ulcers, heart disease and liver trouble.

Doctors studied 14,678 cases and discovered that prejudiced people died earlier than those who were not prejudiced. The nervous system is apparently affected as well as the bile and other organs of the body.

The results of the study show that people who were prejudiced on race, color and religion had a much shorter life-span than people who showed no prejudices. It also indicated that people who had three prejudices a day were far more affected than people who only had one prejudice a day.

It is believed that when the report is released, prejudiced people all over America will protest the findings. They are expected to point out that prejudice is one of the big industries in the United States, and the report could cause unemployment and great financial loss to the economy.

Prejudice gives people pleasure, and anything that gives people pleasure should not be outlawed, the opponents of the report say.

"You can't outlaw prejudice by law," a spokesman for the prejudice industry told me when I discussed the report with him.

"But this is not a moral question, it's a matter of health," I said. "Don't you think people should be warned that they will die much earlier if they are prejudiced?"

"We are conducting a study of our own," the spokesman said. "It's quite possible that the people in the government study would have died anyway. We have many elderly people who are prejudiced and they don't seem to be suffering at all."

"But the big danger of prejudice, according to the report," I said, "is that it can be inherited from one generation to another. Don't you think this is dangerous?"

"It's one of the prices we have to pay for enjoying prejudice. Heck, life wouldn't be worth living if you didn't hate someone."

It is expected that when the report is released there will be an educational program to make people give up prejudice.

A doctor who has been fighting prejudice for years told me, "Of course, we don't expect people to give up all their prejudices. All we ask is for those who wish to continue to do so in moderation. I don't think there is anything wrong in being prejudiced about the weather or your boss or your in-laws. But heavy prejudice will kill you."

VI. THE NERVOUS CANARY

☆☆☆☆☆☆☆☆☆☆☆☆

IT PAYS TO ADVERTISE

There is no question that the cigarette companies are in a tremendous amount of trouble since the government report on smoking. The Federal Trade Commission has indicated it may force the companies to label the cigarette packages with all sorts of warnings, including the tar and nicotine content of each pack.

Will the cigarette companies be able to survive this assault? I believe they will. It's just a question of advertising.

I take you now to the board room of the Frantic Cigarette Company, where the chairman, the advertising agency executives, the vice-president in charge of sales and public relations counselors are going at it hot and heavy.

Chairman of the board: "Gentlemen, have you come up with any ideas since our last meeting?"

"Well, J. L., I think we have to change our brand name. What do you think of calling our cigarettes Blue Cross? It has a nice medical sound to it."

"That's not bad," the chairman of the board says. "It certainly shows we have the smoker's interest at heart."

"J. L.," the advertising manager says, "we've taken a survey and no one seems to know what the tar and nicotine content in a cigarette means, so what I suggest is we play up the tar and nicotine percentages. We could say Blue Cross cigarettes contain twice, yes twice, as much tar as any leading brand. Independent research shows that there is 13 percent more nicotine in a Blue Cross than in any other cigarette. Why pay more for less tar and nicotine when you can smoke Blue Cross?"

J. L. says, "It's a thought."

The advertising manager says, "We've been working on a campaign for television. Our first commercial shows a car

129

going off a cliff. Then we close in on the smashed-up driver, who says, 'If I had been home smoking Blue Cross, this would have never happened!'

"The second commercial shows a mountain climber hanging by a rope from Mt. Everest. He turns to the audience as the rope breaks and shouts, 'Fresh air will kill you!'

"A third commercial shows a girl and a boy on a beach. The boy offers her a Blue Cross and she says, 'I'd rather die.' He tells her she's a poor sport and if he knew she was that kind of a girl he would have never asked her out on a date. 'But I promised my mother,' she says. He makes her take one puff and she begs, 'Please don't hate me.' He says, 'How can I hate someone who smokes Blue Cross?' "

"I like it," says J. L. "Buy the time. Now let's talk about some television shows."

The public relations man says, "We were thinking of serializing Henry Miller's *Tropic of Cancer*. There should be great audience identification there."

"You're sick," J. L. says. "What else?"

"We have a show called *Disaster*. One week we'd deal with an earthquake, the next week a flood, the next week a forest fire. The idea is that there are a lot worse things in the world than smoking."

"That sounds all right," J. L. says. "But I still would like to know whose idea it was to put on the *Life of Madame Curie* last week."

"He's been fired, J. L."

"Now, gentlemen, we're fighting for our lives, and we're going to need every one of you if we're going to save the company."

"We're with you, J. L.," they shout.

"Not so fast. In order to win this fight and keep all of you on your toes, I'm issuing a new rule. No one in the organization will be allowed to smoke."

"But J. L.—"

"You heard what I said," J. L. says. "The company comes first, and if we're going to sell cigarettes, I don't want a lot of sick people on my hands."

HE GAVE THEM UP

The trouble with giving up smoking is there never seems to be a right moment to do it. One day I was in Chicago ready to fly

"That's the trouble around here," I shouted. "Nobody thinks they're doing anything wrong. I have news for you. I've got hostile feelings, too."

"Well, who said you didn't?" she said as she went into the kitchen and slammed the door.

I was starting to feel better already.

An hour later we all sat down to dinner.

"Please pass the potatoes, Dad," my nine-year-old son said.

"What are you interrupting for?" I yelled.

"All I said was 'Please pass the potatoes.' "

"That can be considered an interruption."

"Now, don't start on him," my wife warned.

"I'm fed up with being Mr. Nice Guy around here. First he asks for the potatoes, next he'll ask for money, then he'll want to go out with girls, and pretty soon he'll be drinking and smoking. Somebody has to speak up. He'll thank me someday for not passing the potatoes."

After dinner I started punching the pillows on the couch. Then the doorbell rang.

The boy collecting money for the newspaper was standing there.

"What do you want?" I demanded.

"The money for the newspaper," he replied.

"I don't have any money. Now, what are you going to do about that?" And I slammed the door.

Thirty minutes later the doorbell rang again.

The paper boy was there with his father.

"Why don't you pay the kid for delivering your papers?" the father wanted to know.

"He can't fight his own battles, huh? I thought he was yellow."

"What do you mean, yellow? Let's step out here and see who's yellow."

"I'm not stepping outside to fight the father of some kid who can't fight his own battles."

For the rest of the evening I vented my hostility against my mother-in-law, who telephoned, a neighbor who wanted us for dinner, and a woman collecting money for the American Red Cross.

The next day I called the doctor.

"All bets are off," I informed him.

"Why?" he wanted to know.

"My son ran away from home, my wife is packing her bags,

I can't get morning newspapers anymore, someone's father
wants to sock me in the jaw, none of the neighbors are talking
to me, my mother-in-law is going to visit me because she fears
for the safety of the children, and I've just been marked lousy
because I wouldn't give to the American Red Cross."

"I see what you mean," the doctor said. "Maybe you better
take up golf instead."

I looked at the phone in disbelief. "Now you tell me?"

THE NERVOUS CANARY

I read once that a psychiatrist had just completed a study on
pets in the home and had discovered that neurotic families
had neurotic pets. That is to say, the pets became neurotic.

The psychiatrist said he had studied dogs, cats, parakeets and
other pets and he noticed that they all tended to take on the
characteristics of their masters. If the master was nervous, the
dog was nervous; if the mother screamed, the parrot screamed,
and so forth.

As the father of a rabbit, two hamsters and a canary, I was
very interested in the report and I tried to fit it into my particular situation.

For example, the day after I read the report, I heard my
wife screaming: "How many times do I have to ask you people
to come to dinner?"

"Hush, Mother," I said, "you're making the canary nervous."

"I don't care about the canary. I want everybody at the
dinner table when dinner is ready."

The canary started flying back and forth across the cage.

"You see," I said, "you've made the canary neurotic."

"I haven't made the canary neurotic," she said. "That canary
was neurotic when we got him."

"That's not true," I said. "According to a distinguished
psychiatrist, household pets become neurotic only in neurotic
homes."

Just then my nine-year-old daughter arrived with one of her
hamsters.

"How many times have I told you not to bring your hamster
to the table?" my wife said.

The hamster started to quiver.

"You see," I said, "the hamster is filled with anxieties."

"Are you trying to say I'm neurotic because I don't like to eat with a hamster?" my wife said.

"All I'm telling you is what the psychiatrist found out. There must be something to it. We have a canary who won't sing, two hamsters who quiver every time you get near them and a rabbit who just sits in the corner all day and doesn't say anything."

My ten-year-old son arrived at the table.

"Have you been playing with the rabbit?" my wife demanded.

He said, "Yes."

"Then go wash your hands. I've told you a million times."

The canary started scratching on the cage.

"There," I said, "don't tell me that canary is happy."

"Has it ever occurred to your psychiatrist-expert that household pets can make people neurotic?" my wife said.

"It isn't possible."

"Then why am I quivering?" she demanded.

"Do you think it's possible that you've taken on the characteristics of the children's pets?"

"I don't really know," she said, scratching her nose against the canary's cage.

"Mother," I cried, "you've made medical history."

"DON'T INHALE—JUST PUFF"

It is very rare that a minority can win a battle for freedom overnight. But I've seen it happen right here in the United States. The minority I'm talking about are the cigar smokers of America, of which I happen to be a member. Up until recently cigar smokers were treated as lepers. We were insulted by hostesses, pushed around by airline stewardesses, held in contempt by children and persecuted by our wives.

Even the movies gave cigar smokers a bad image. Only crooked politicians and gangsters smoked cigars in films. But despite the persecution we cigar smokers stuck to our guns, or whatever other people called them. Many times we had to choose between cigars and people and we always chose cigars, because they lasted longer and we could enjoy them more.

It was a lonely life, but I pursued it for the pleasure it gave me. If you're going to have a vice, it might as well be one that society doesn't approve of.

And then it happened. The Surgeon General's report on

cigarettes was issued and all of a sudden cigar smokers were in and cigarette smokers were out. Cigar smoking, the S. G. report said, had little effect on cancer, and cigar smokers were slated to live much longer than cigarette smokers.

Overnight people who would have nothing to do with me before sought me out and asked, "Would you teach me how to smoke a cigar?"

"Don't inhale, jerk," I would scream in the first lesson. "Just puff."

"But how can you smoke without inhaling?" was the inevitable question.

"When you smoke a cigar, you're going for oral satisfaction, not for smoke in your lungs."

It was hard work, but I taught many cigarette smokers how to puff a cigar.

Not only was I sought after as a cigar-smoking teacher, but suddenly I was in demand socially. Hostesses would introduce me by saying, "I want you to meet Mr. Buchwald. He smoked cigars before the Surgeon General's report came out."

People were immediately impressed and several asked for my autograph for their children.

Puffing happily on a corona, I tried to act modestly.

"It's really nothing. I had a feeling about cigarettes when I was ten years old. The kids in the neighborhood used to smoke cigarettes behind the railroad tracks, and I noted they started coughing. It occurred to me that there was a correlation between cigarettes and coughing. So at ten years old I started smoking cigars."

The best part of being a cigar smoker is that women are now smoking cigars and I'm constantly being approached by beautiful women at parties who say, "My, your cigar smells good. I wonder if I could have one?"

I usually blush and hand them one. Some of them whisper, "I like you."

"But I'm not handsome," I reply.

"I know," they say. "But you're going to live longer."

And so all the years of unhappiness have finally paid off. Thanks to the Surgeon General, cigar smokers can now puff in peace, blowing smoke in the faces of the very people who persecuted them for years.

VII. STATUS SYMBOLS
☆☆☆☆☆☆☆☆☆☆☆☆☆☆☆☆☆☆☆☆☆☆☆☆☆☆

JOHN GOLDFARB, 1945

As an alumnus of the University of Southern California, the only team to beat Notre Dame this year, I was sorry to see Notre Dame get an injunction against 20th Century-Fox over the film *John Goldfarb, Please Come Home*.

In the film, John Goldfarb, an American U-2 pilot, crashes in an Arab country and is forced to coach a football team that is going to play Notre Dame. On the eve of the game the Notre Dame football players are treated to an orgy of eating, drinking and belly dancers, and the next day they lose to the Arabs.

As I read the plot it had a familiar ring to it and suddenly I realized why.

It was October, 1945, and for the lack of enough combat points I was stuck in the U. S. Marine Corps indefinitely. The only thing that made life worth living in those days was that I had managed to get a job as publicity director of the Cherry Point (N. C.) Marine Corps football team. The team was lousy, but the food was good, and I was minding my own business when I suddenly received an urgent call to go to Washington. It seems Cherry Point was slated to play the Air Transport Command, and the Marine Corps brass, now that the war was over, was determined to win.

When I arrived, four generals and six colonels asked me for a rundown on the Cherry Point team. Not wanting to disappoint them, I was very optimistic about our chances, so much so that the Marine Corps officers were giving their Air Force friends 14 points, and betting a month's salary.

I was a little nervous about their enthusiasm, but as a sergeant I was in no position to dampen it.

The publicity on the game, if I must say so myself, was

excellent, and according to the papers the Cherry Point team sounded like a military version of the Green Bay Packers. Pretty soon the Marine Corps command was giving 21 points and finding it hard to get takers.

The game was scheduled for Sunday and the team arrived on Saturday by bus, raring to tear the Air Force team to shreds. I took them to their hotel and in the course of talking to them about Washington I mentioned there were many pretty girls in the town.

Most of the players had just come back from the Pacific and didn't know what girls were, so I had to explain to them. When I did, the members of the team said, "That's for us."

"But you've got to play tomorrow," I said.

Two tackles and three guards started shaking me. "We want whatever you call them."

In a few hours the hotel suite looked like the key scene from *John Goldfarb*.

The chandeliers were swinging, the windows were rattling and the roof of the hotel was about to blow off. The party lasted until six in the morning and some of the players decided to get dressed in their football uniforms since it was so near kickoff time.

That afternoon the only Marines on the field who could stand up straight were the U. S. Marine Corps band. The Cherry Point Marines were defeated, I believe 36-0, but my only memory of the day was the looks on the faces of the Marine Corps officers in the stands, who had bet against the Air Force team.

After the game the team got on the bus and slept all the way to Cherry Point. The next day I was called in and told because of my fine war record they were going to discharge me ahead of time. It was either that or a court-martial.

It was a pretty sad story, but when you think about it, it would make a helluva movie. I wonder if 20th Century-Fox would be interested?

WHAT FATHERS WANT
FOR CHRISTMAS

Kids these days have no appreciation of the real value of Christmas. All they talk about is how many presents they're going to get. None of them is aware of the sacrifices fathers have made to make their Christmas a pleasant one. We fathers don't want much in exchange. All we ask is that our sons let us play with their toys on Christmas morning.

Last Christmas I bought my ten-year-old son an electric racing car set. It looked like a real speedway and came complete with a scaled model of a Ferrari and a Lotus racing car. There were banked curves, bridges, fences and pits. You couldn't ask for a better present.

Christmas morning I said to my son, "How about playing with your racing cars? We could have a race."

"I don't want to," he said, unwrapping an aircraft carrier.

"What do you mean, you don't want to? You know how much that thing cost?"

He was adamant. "I don't want to play with them now."

"He doesn't want to play with his cars," I said to my wife.

"It's his Christmas," she said. "Let him play with what he wants to."

"You're always taking his side," I complained.

"Play with the cars yourself," she said.

"It's no fun. You have to have two to race."

The boy opened a fort I had especially selected. I started placing soldiers in it.

"I don't want the soldiers placed like that," he whined.

"That's the way they should be placed," I said. "I wasn't in the Marines for nothing."

"I want them another way."

"I said they should go like that."

He ran off to complain to his mother. She said, "Why don't you let him put the soldiers in the fort the way he wants to?"

"All the soldiers will get killed if he does," I said.

"Well, that's his business. Why don't you open up your own presents?"

I opened up a box and all that was in it was a cashmere pullover sweater.

My son opened up another gift to find a hockey game.

"Let's play a game of hockey," I said excitedly. "I used to play it when I was a kid."

"I'm waiting for Butch to come over," he said. "I'll play it with him."

"What does Butch know about hockey?" I cried.

My wife gave me another box. It contained a wallet.

"Open up that package," I told my son. It contained a gas-oline-driven airplane that cost me $14.

The boy took over the airplane. "I wonder how it works," he said.

"I'll show you," I said. "Let's go outside."

"It's too cold," he replied. "We'll fly it tomorrow."

I was just about to grab the plane when I got a call from my friend, Ed Williams.

"How's your Christmas?" he wanted to know.

"Lousy. How's yours?"

"The same. Jobie won't even let me play with his rock collection."

"I got an idea. I'll send Joel over there to play with Jobie's toys, and you come over here and we'll play with Joel's toys."

"Do you have a racing car set?"

"Of course."

"I'll be right over. Can I have the Ferrari?"

KEEPING UP WITH THE JONESES

According to everything you read, every one in the United States is trying to keep up with the Joneses. Economists will tell you, if it weren't for people keeping up with the Joneses, the country would go into a tailspin and there would be widespread unemployment and a recession of monumental proportions.

Therefore, the Joneses are very important to this nation and could be considered our most valuable natural resource.

You would think every one named Jones would be happy to be the pace setters of America, but such is not the case, at least not in my neighborhood. Just the other day I interviewed Mr. and Mrs. Jones, whom every one in my area is constantly living up to, and it was a very enlightening talk.

Mr. Jones was just laying out a carpet of grass in front of his house. "It's the latest thing," he said. "You don't need grass seed anymore. I suppose every one on the block will be copying me soon."

"You must feel pretty good to be the pace setter in the neighborhood," I said.

"Well," he replied, "it's a grave responsibility keeping ahead of everybody all the time. And it's expensive, too. But you kinda get used to it. Come on inside and have a bullshot."

"What's a bullshot?"

"It's vodka and consommé—the latest drink."

I went inside and was introduced to Mrs. Jones, who was watching color television on a 40-inch set.

"Fella here wants to interview us on how it feels to be named Jones," Mr. Jones told his wife.

Mrs. Jones said, "I hope you told him we're getting fed up."

"Now, Miriam."

"Well, if you won't tell him, I will," she said angrily. "It's getting to be a bore. Oh, I'll admit in the beginning I enjoyed it. Everyone admired us, everyone envied us, everyone tried to emulate us. But it's so hard to stay ahead."

"How do you mean, Mrs. Jones?"

"We were the first ones in the neighborhood to own two cars. Then everyone bought two automobiles to keep up with us. So we had to buy a third one and build a three-car garage. Now the people across the street have three cars, so we're going to have to buy a fourth one. It's getting too much."

"Hush, Miriam," said Mr. Jones, "you have to put the country first. If we didn't buy a fourth car, just think what would happen to the automobile industry. Detroit is depending on us."

"I don't care about Detroit," Mrs. Jones said. "Did you tell him about our swimming pool? We put in a swimming pool. Three months later there were seven swimming pools in the area, so we had to come up with something new. We installed an outdoor kitchen in the patio. Now everybody has an outdoor kitchen in their patios. What else can we put there?"

"We're going to install a Finnish steam bath," Mr. Jones said. "No one around here has one."

"And then what?" Mrs. Jones asked. "Last year we went to Europe. This year every one is going to Europe, so now we have to go to the Far East."

"We've got a tiger hunt planned in Nepal for next year," Mr. Jones said.

"I'm so sick and tired of traveling," Mrs. Jones complained. "Why can't people keep up with somebody else? All I seem to be doing is packing and unpacking, throwing parties I can't afford, buying Cassini gowns, sending my children to the best private schools, and redecorating the house every month. I'd rather live the life of Riley."

"Now, Miriam," Mr. Jones said. "You shouldn't talk like that in front of this here reporter, or he'll get the impression we're un-American."

"I'm going upstairs and take a Lasterperin," Mrs. Jones said.

"What's that?" I asked Mr. Jones.

"It's the latest thing in headache powders. Works seven times as fast as aspirin."

SIT DOWN SO YOU DON'T
ROCK THE BOAT

After covering all the resorts in Europe for the past fifteen years, I was curious to visit an American resort. So I went up to Grossinger's at the foot of the Catskill Mountains in New York and I must say there is nothing like it in Europe.

Grossinger's is not just a resort—it's a way of life. From morning until night the guests are coddled, amused, lectured, and entertained. There is nothing Grossinger's won't do for a client.

The first person I met when I arrived at Grossinger's was Mr. Lou Goldstein, who is in charge of all guest activities.

I noticed Grossinger's had golf courses, tennis courts, volleyball, bowling alleys, swimming pools, etc., etc., and since I'd been active in Pierre Salinger's Anti-Physical Fitness Program, I became a little nervous.

But Mr. Goldstein assured me the athletic facilities had nothing to do with the guests. "We put them there," he said, "because we have a lot of land we don't know what to do with. If you're like the other guests, you won't be on your feet more than ten minutes the entire day."

"Well, what do you do then?" I asked.

"In the morning, you sit down for breakfast in the dining room. Then you walk—all downhill—to the terrace where I put on an hour's show of jokes and laughs. After the show there is calisthenics. I give finger exercises for people who are going to play gin rummy and canasta in the afternoon.

"Then I hold up a three-pound medicine ball and I let each person touch it."

"What happens next?" I asked excitedly.

"Then you rest up for the walk to the couch in the lobby where you prepare yourself for the most strenuous activity of the day—which is eating lunch.

"After lunch if you're not too tired, and don't want to take a nap, you go to the pool where you sit in a chaise chair while we put on a diving show for you. Not everyone likes to watch it because you have to move your head up and down.

"When the show is over we all go over to the dance studio to sit and watch a dance lesson.

"Then you go back to your couch in the lobby to rest up before going upstairs to change for dinner. After sitting in the cocktail lounge, you sit in the dining room and then you go into the nightclub, and sit and watch the show."

"That's very nice," I said. "Pierre Salinger would give this hotel a very good rating."

"Of course," Mr. Goldstein said, "there are some physical fitness fanatics here, and we're at their service too. For instance, if you want to throw the horseshoe, one of our staff picks it up for you, cleans it, and hands it back to you. All you have to do is throw it again.

"If you want to play ping-pong and you feel it's too exhausting, we'll remove the net.

"If you want to play baseball, your busboy will run the bases for you.

"We also have an exercise rowing machine in the health club and for $2 an hour we'll get a bellboy to row for you."

"You've sold me," I said.

"We believe in catering to the guests," he said. "Unfortunately, the more activities you have for the guests, the more spoiled they become. A few weeks ago, on the day of the eclipse, a lady came outside and saw it was very cloudy, and so she said to me, 'Mr. Goldstein, are you going to cancel the eclipse today?' "

AN INEXPENSIVE SUMMER

Many people are wondering how to have an inexpensive summer vacation. I'm happy to tell you how to do it because I feel that since I've been able to do it anybody can.

In the beginning I decided that the best way to save money was not to go away.

"Our house is air-conditioned," my wife said, "and lots of people stay in Washington."

"Exactly my thoughts," I said. "We'll stay home. What should we do with the children?"

"We can send them to day camp up the street. They'll love it."

So we enrolled the three children in day camp at $25 a week per child. It was a small investment and certainly worth it.

In the meantime I decided I should take up tennis, so I joined a tennis club for $150 a season.

Everything was going along fine until the weekends.

"The children don't have anything to do on weekends," my wife complained.

"What do you suggest?" I asked.

"Why don't we join the pool at the Sheraton Park Hotel? It's only $100 for the two months," she suggested. "Then they can go swimming on the weekends."

"Good idea. It's still cheaper than going away," I said.

"Oh, by the way, as long as we're staying home, I need some patio furniture," she said.

"What kind of patio furniture?"

"About $200 worth."

"That seems like a lot for patio furniture."

"Well, if we're going to stay home, we have to have a nice-looking patio."

"I guess you're right."

"I'll call the electrician tomorrow."

"The electrician?"

"Yes, I want him to hang up some lights in the garden. I saw some wonderful globes that looked exactly like moons. They're not expensive. Installed they cost only $150. Will you be home tomorrow when he's here?"

"No," I said. "I just joined the Washington Athletic Club so I could take a swim at lunchtime."

"How much is that?" she wanted to know.

"Just $100. It's worth it."

A week went by and then my wife said, "Joel wants to go away to a real camp. He says day camps aren't any fun."

"Where shall we send him?"

"I found a lovely camp in western Pennsylvania. It's only $500 for the season."

Joel was shipped off to camp. But this didn't go over very well with the girls. My wife said, "They're mad that Joel has gone away."

"Shall we send them to camp, also?"

"They don't want to go," she said.

"Thank goodness," I said. "That saves us $1,000."

"Not exactly," my wife said. "Day camp ends in July. They have nothing to do in August."

"What about the pool?"

"It's always crowded. I thought we might put in our own pool. I saw one advertised in the papers for $3,000."

"Put it in," I shouted. "We can't have our kids with nothing to do in August."

"I knew you'd see it my way. I'll have to call up the electrician."

"What for?"

"To take down all the globes."

So far I've spent only $7,000 staying at home, and we have only eight weeks to go. I figure that if someone follows my plan they can have a wonderful time and it will cost them as little as $10,000 for the summer. When you can do it for that, it hardly seems worth going away at all.

THE GUEST STEALERS

Not long ago, I wrote about building a swimming pool. I thought all my problems would be over once it was built, but I was wrong. One of the things I had been warned about was that as soon as I had a pool I would be terribly bothered by people who wanted to use it. This, unfortunately, has turned out to be untrue.

I have had a hard time getting people to come over to see it, much less use it. The only real enjoyment in owning a pool is showing it off to less fortunate people than yourself. To make it pay off you have to have guests who admire it, ogle it, and tell you how lucky you are. It's no fun to sit by your pool alone or even to use it for a swim if no one knows you have it at the back of your house.

The trouble in Washington is that so many people have pools now that you're vying for each other's guests. Before I had my pool I was on very good terms with the David Brinkleys. They had a pool and it didn't take much to get me to come over to their house. But since I built my pool, I keep turning down their invitations to come over and now they're hardly speaking to me. It's true they had their pool first, but I can't afford to leave my pool, even for an afternoon, when I've got so much invested in it.

In order to attract guests, I put in an outdoor bar, have guaranteed lunch and dinner, and I present each person with an autographed copy of my book when they leave.

As an added attraction I bought a trampoline diving board

at great expense. And yet, when the weekend comes, I still have trouble getting guests. Most of them, I discover, are going over to the Brinkleys' or the Bobby Kennedys' or to the White House for a swim.

You only have to build a pool to know who your real friends are. Take the Phil Geyelins. He works for the *Wall Street Journal* and lives around the corner from me. I could always count on the Geyelins coming over to the house and we had a wonderful, warm relationship.

Then, behind my back, without any warning, they decided to build their own pool. They tried to pretend they built it for their children, but I knew it was done out of spite. To add insult to injury they invited me over to *their* place for a swim.

You can imagine what I told them. And if that wasn't enough, I've heard through the grapevine that they invited several people that I had intended to invite for this weekend. Between them and the Brinkleys, I have hardly any guest list left.

This kind of thing has been going on all summer. As soon as you get a guest lined up, someone else steals him from you.

Another thing that has spoiled things for me is that Washington has been unusually cool and many people who might ordinarily be interested in coming for a swim say they'd rather take a drive in the country.

I've even offered to take the Brinkley overflow, but they're so mad at me that when their pool fills up they send the people over to the Averell Harrimans, which is much farther away.

If I had known how difficult it was to get people to use my swimming pool, I might never have built it. Maybe I'll open it to the USO.

LEAVES OF GRASS

The Commerce Department revealed last May that Americans spend $1.5 billion on their lawns. The figure isn't hard to believe if you own a lawn. As a matter of fact, it's quite low. All you have to do is to buy a few feet of sod, some fertilizer, some grass seed, a hose, and an electric lawn mower, and you've blown a million right there.

No one is quite sure who was the first one to start the lawn competition in America. It is rumored that it was a Pilgrim named Sam Snodgrass who was responsible for the whole thing.

One morning the Pilgrims got up and found Sam out front sprinkling seeds on the ground.

"What art thou doing, Sam?" his neighbors asked.

"Planting grass."

"But why? Canst thou eat it?"

"No, neighbor, but it will give me something to cut in the summertime."

The Pilgrim men, who rarely laughed, made merry of Sam. But when spring came and Sam's lawn started to grow, the wives of the other Pilgrims became very upset.

"Look, thou, at Brother Snodgrass' lawn," they said to their husbands. "It is verily a shame that we have nothing but dirt in front of our houses."

The other Pilgrim men were sore as hell, but there wasn't much they could do about it. So they all started planting grass in front of their houses. Pretty soon they were so busy working on their lawns they forgot to plant any crops and when winter came they almost starved to death.

But this did not dismay the Pilgrim wives. When spring came, they insisted that their husbands work on their lawns again.

"Look thee at Sam, with nary a weed in his yard," they grumbled.

"Women," the husbands cried, "we must plant crops instead."

"Better to starve," the women replied, "than to have an unkempt lawn."

And so the next winter all the Pilgrims died. But the tradition of having a neat lawn lived on in the New World and America became a great nation because the wives of its men always thought the grass was greener on the other side of the hedge.

Today a man is judged by the lawn he keeps. If it is trim and green and looks like a carpet, he is a loyal American. If it grows tall, has weeds, and straggles over on the sidewalk, he is a Communist.

And so once again this past spring, from the Atlantic to the Pacific, American men, egged on by their wives, were toiling in their front yards, devoting their strength, their lives, and their waking moments, not to mention $1.5 billion a year, to keep up with their neighbors' lawns.

The Pilgrims started it, but where it will all end, sod only knows.

DEBUTANTE PARTY

There was a time when debutante parties used to be covered by
society editors, but now they have to be covered by police reporters. Following the famous Wanamaker party on Long
Island last summer, eight young blue bloods were just found
guilty of wrecking a cottage in Towson, Maryland, a suburb of
Baltimore. The party after the Maryland Hunt Ball caused
$1,800 in damage as compared to the $6,000 damage in South-
ampton, which proves that the Long Island set still gives the
better parties.

If the trend continues, this is how a debutante party story
will read on the society pages:

Miss Mary Jane Merryweather made her debut at the Piping
Hot Country Club last night with 1,200 guests in attendance.
Following a supper dance given by her parents, the party
moved over to the rented home of Mr. Chauncey Hogglesworth, where the young socialites enjoyed themselves until
dawn.

Among the guests were Miss Hilary Weepingwillow, wearing a Christian Dior gown, and her escort, Robert Goosepimple III. Mr. Goosepimple, a four-letter man at Harvard,
gave a demonstration of his prowess by swinging from a
chandelier 14 times across the room before it broke.

George "Laddie" Goldstuff, Jr., scion to a pillowmaking
fortune, and his lovely partner, Hilda Mayberry, climbed the
drapes to get a better view of the party. They were joined by
Edward Trojan and "Sissy" Carpenter of Bryn Mawr. Punch
was served up to the two couples from a rare Baccarat vase
that had been in the Hogglesworth family for over 100 years.

A great deal of laughter ensued when Mr. Goldstuff threw
the vase out of the window after drinking the punch. What
made the incident most amusing was that the window was
closed.

Dancing on the fireplace mantel were Rodney Ruggles and
Jeannie Wimple, of the breadcrumb Wimples. While twisting,
Jeannie lost her balance, but was saved from falling by grab-
bing a Cézanne painting which was hanging over the mantel.
The painting was irreparably damaged, but thanks to Jeannie's
quick thinking, she wasn't.

As the party went on, it became more exciting. A touch football game was started in the dining room, and in place of a football the players used Mr. Hogglesworth's Wedgwood plates. Every time someone missed a pass the spectators cheered. The game lasted until there were no plates left.

While many couples were enjoying themselves on the ground floor, a group of merrymakers went upstairs and started throwing furniture out the window. Shouts of glee could be heard from the upper floors as the furniture crashed to the ground.

Then someone remembered that it was time for breakfast, so a fire was built in the library and several of the partygoers fried ham and eggs over it, which the famished guests ate with delight.

When no napkins could be found, Nancy Lou Fingerer cut up curtains from the windows. Despite her wealthy background, Nancy is a wonderful homemaker.

As dawn came up, the band played "Auld Lang Syne" and the couples started departing.

Everyone agreed it was probably the best debutante party of the season and one that they would all remember for years to come.

As Mr. Goldstuff, Sr., said to the District Attorney the next morning, "These kids deserve a little clean fun before they grow up, and I'd rather know where they are than have them roaming the streets."

FATHER OF THE YEAR

I have just been named Literary Father of the Year by the National Father's Day Committee. It is the highest honor any writer in America can receive, just one notch above the Pulitzer Prize, and I'm very humble about it.

This is how the honor came about. Most Washington newspapermen fathers are rarely ever home. In checking down the list, the committee discovered I averaged at least two and a half days a week at home, which was a record for someone in my business. Any newspaperman who sees his kids that often has to be the Father of the Year.

The honor came to me when I was on a trip to the West Coast for a lecture swing. My wife and children were so excited, they called me right away.

"You've just been named Father of the Year," my wife said. "I thought you'd like to know."

"I knew I was up for it," I said, "but I was afraid Sonny Liston would beat me out in the finals."

"When are you coming home, Daddy?" my son asked on the extension.

"I must be out another week," I told him. "I have speeches to make all over the country."

"You're always away," he complained.

"That shows how much you know. If I wasn't away so much, I would have never been elected Father of the Year. They don't give these awards to nobodies. They give them to successful persons."

"What's a successful person?"

"That's somebody who is never home."

My daughter got on the phone. "Are you going to bring us any presents?"

"Of course I am. What kind of a Father of the Year do you take me for?"

"If you come home right now, you don't have to bring any presents," she said.

"I can't come home and you know it. Why can't you kids get anything straight?"

"You don't have to shout at them," my wife said.

"I'm not shouting," I shouted. "Here I am, trying to make a living, and all I ever get from anyone is when are you coming home?"

My wife said, "It's not a bad question when you come to think of it."

"I have a good mind not to go to New York and pick up the award."

"You mean you have to go to New York to get the award?"

"Of course I do. They won't give it to you if you don't show up for the luncheon."

"That means you'll be away again."

"You don't understand. In order to be worthy of the award, you have to earn it. You have to be seen around. People have to get to know you. Who's going to know you're Father of the Year material if you spend all your time with your family?"

THE PRICE OF A SWIMMING POOL

As part of my war on poverty I decided to install a swimming pool in a new house I bought. I didn't realize how complicated the purchase of a swimming pool can be. Next to used-car dealers, swimming-pool salesmen are the most sincere of all business men, and one tends to believe everything they tell you.

I interviewed a swimming-pool salesman and you can't imagine what an education it was.

After looking over the property he said, "I can put in a pool—complete—for $8,400."

"That includes everything?" I asked.

"Of course. That's my price—complete."

"Well, it is a little high," I said, "but perhaps I can make it. I'd like a rectangular pool."

"A rectangular pool? I wish you had told me that before. That's $600 extra. You see, it's very difficult to dig a rectangle in the ground."

"That brings it up to $9,000," I said.

"Yes, but that will be complete with everything. Now I'd like to ask you a few questions."

"Yes, sir."

"Did you plan on putting water in the pool?" he asked.

"I thought it would be fun."

"That will be an extra $250. You see, if we put water in the pool, we have to get a permit from the District of Columbia and that takes a great deal of time."

"I knew I shouldn't have asked for water," I said.

"Did you want concrete in the pool?"

"I think so. Why do you ask?"

"Well, the pool gets so muddy otherwise. The concrete will be $350 extra. Of course, if you want Gunite, it will be $500."

"What's the difference?"

"If you use regular concrete, the pool will leak."

He wrote everything down in his book.

"Let me ask you this," he continued. "Had you planned on filtering the water?"

"I guess so. What are the advantages?"

"Well, if you filter the water, there is less chance of the

children's catching typhoid or yellow fever. We can give you an excellent filter for $450."

"I guess in the long run it would be cheaper," I said.

"Now what about the steps to get out of the pool?"

"Couldn't the people just climb over the side?" I inquired.

"They could, but that would mean we'd have to build coping around the pool. The steps cost $200, the coping $550."

"You'd better give us steps."

"What had you planned to put around the pool?" he asked.

"I don't know. What do you put around the pool?"

"We could give you a concrete walk for $670."

"It sounds like you're losing money on the job," I said.

"That's our problem," he replied. "Now what about tree leaves in the pool?"

"I don't want any leaves in the pool," I said, hoping to save some money.

"We don't put leaves in the pool," he said. "We take them out. You'll want a skimmer for $320. Did you plan on having a diving board?"

"Sure, why not?"

"That will be $1,000," he said.

"A thousand dollars for a diving board?" I asked incredulously.

"Not just for the diving board," he said. "If you're going to have a diving board, you'll need deep water. The price I gave you was for a shallow pool. I thought you understood that. Why don't you get anything I say straight?"

"I'm sorry," I apologized. "Will you ever forgive me?"

He wrote down $1,000 in his notebook. "Just this once. But let's have no more haggling."

STATUS SYMBOL

The latest status symbol in Hollywood is a telephone in your automobile. Anybody who is anybody has one, and it certainly fulfills a function. If, for example, you go into a drive-in movie at night, you can call the baby-sitter without leaving.

If you're driving while drunk, you can call Alcoholics Anonymous and they'll send you a tow car to talk you out of it. If you want to get out of a date, you can always call up and say you're tied up in traffic.

A friend of mine, Bill Dana, who plays Jose Jimenez on

television, has a phone in his Cadillac and one day I decided to call him. But I didn't have his number, so I called the phone company and said, "I'd like the number of Bill Dana. He was last seen driving a black Cadillac down the San Diego Freeway."

The operator came back in a few minutes and said, "I'm sorry, he has an unlisted number."

Having an unlisted phone in your car is about as high on the status hog as you can get.

"Well, do you know of any cars with phones near him who might give him a message?" I asked.

"I'm sorry. You might try the telephone answering service. It's a Greyhound bus that drives around town taking messages for mobile telephones."

I called the answering service and they said Mr. Dana would probably cross Hollywood and Vine in 20 minutes and they'd give him the message.

Sure enough, 20 minutes later Mr. Dana called me.

But before I could tell him what I wanted, he said, "Could I call back? I've got Cary Grant on 'hold.'"

Five minutes later he called again. "I'm sorry I've been so busy, but everyone seems to be calling me today."

"Where are you now?" I asked him.

"At Vermont and Wilshire. I had to call my agent and I was getting very bad reception on Vine Street."

"How come you have an unlisted number in your car?" I asked him.

"I don't want everyone to call me at all hours of the night. I might have a girl in the car."

"I never thought of that."

"Where are you calling from?" he wanted to know.

"The Beverly Wilshire Hotel," I said.

"Well, let me drive nearer there and I'll save a dime in toll charges. I'll call you back."

"Listen, Bill. The reason I called is—"

"Can you hold on a second? I have to buy some gas."

I held on for a few moments and he was back. "Sorry, there's someone at the door."

"At the door?"

"Yeah, a cop. He wants to give me a ticket for dialing too fast. He says I was dialing 60 in a 55 area code."

"What are you going to do?"

"I'll call my lawyer in his Thunderbird as soon as I finish speaking to you."

"Bill, what I wanted to know was—"

The operator interrupted. "I'm sorry, your three minutes are up."

"I haven't any more dimes," Dana said.

"Do you have a pay phone in your car?!!"

"Of course. Otherwise everyone on the Freeway would use it."

VIII. THAT'S SHOW BIZ

☆☆☆☆☆☆☆☆☆☆☆☆☆☆☆☆☆☆☆☆☆☆☆☆☆☆

THE KARATE EXPERT

Every once in a while I hear a true story that is so sad I can hardly write it. The other day I heard one about a friend of mine who lives in California. I shall call him Jake Kilduff to protect his identity.

Jake, who works in motion pictures, took up the sport of "karate" about ten years ago. Karate is a Japanese defense system in which the use of the hands plays the major role. Calluses are built up on the hand in such a way that an experienced karate expert can break a brick or a two-by-four by just bringing the edge of his hand down on it.

Let it be said that Jake was in the class with the experts. He was a "black belt," which is pretty high in karate hierarchy and, while other husbands watched television or read *Playboy*, Jake used to spend his time in the cellar breaking blocks of wood with his hand.

Jake's wife thought it was a lot of foolishness and a waste of money (he had invested $3,000 in karate lessons) and every once in a while she'd yell down to the cellar, "Will you stop breaking those bricks with your hand and come to bed?"

"Someday, Mother," he said, "you're going to be happy I know karate. It is the greatest self-defense ever devised by man."

After ten years went by Jake started to doubt he would have a chance to use his skills. But then the big day came.

He was driving along a Los Angeles freeway on a Sunday afternoon with his wife when a sports car cut in front of Jake. Jake got mad and cut in front of the sports car. The man in the sports car got mad and cut in front of Jake.

Pretty soon they were shouting at each other and the man in the sports car yelled, "Pull off the freeway and I'll punch you in the nose."

Jake was elated. All the years of practice and expense were finally going to pay off. His wife begged him to ignore the other man, but Jake just rubbed his calluses against his chin and said, "Is he going to be in for a surprise!"

Jake pulled off the freeway and parked on a stretch of grass. The sports car driver pulled up in front of him and parked. The driver jumped out of his car and started walking toward Jake.

Jake studied him calmly. He was of medium build, not particularly heavy. It would probably take only one slash across the throat with his hand.

The driver moved forward, his right fist held back. "The guy is leaving himself wide open," Jake thought to himself. "Well, he asked for it."

Jake reached down to unfasten his car safety belt. It was stuck. He tried to unfasten it again. It was still stuck. The man reached Jake's car. Jake fought the belt desperately, but to no avail. The driver of the other car reached into the window and hit Jake in the mouth, knocking out two teeth.

As Jake continued to get his belt free, the man returned to his car, got back in, and drove off.

Jake's wife told us it took a week before Jake would even talk to her, and a month before he got a new bridge for his mouth. He's given up karate now. As a matter of fact, every time he sees a two-by-four or a brick, he gets sick to his stomach.

I DIDN'T GET THE NAME

Being in the business I'm in, it's very difficult to remember names. Sometimes it's embarrassing, occasionally it's distressing, and once in a while it can be fatal.

One morning I was riding the Long Island Rail Road's Cannonball from Westhampton to New York when I happened to sit in the parlor car across from a man whose face seemed familiar. He recognized me immediately and said, "This certainly is a coincidence. I've been meaning to call you for some time."

"I've been meaning to call you, too," I said, trying desperately to think who he was.

"We've been talking about a television series based on your columns from Paris."

"That's nice," I replied. Maybe we met at Maxim's or the Hotel George V.

"How's what's-her-name?" I asked, hoping it would give me a clue.

"Oh, we got a divorce two years ago. I'm married again," he said.

"That's interesting. You still living in the same place?"

"No," he said, "we moved to Westhampton. Now about this show. We've got lots of money and we're looking for new ideas."

"Gee, that's neat," I said. Could I have gone to school with him? He seemed about my age.

"This is what we're prepared to offer you. A thousand dollars a show and 10 percent of the profits."

Perhaps if I knew who he worked for something would click. "The company sounds like it's doing well," I said.

"Just great," he said.

"Your offices still in the same building?" I said.

"Same place," he replied. "The thing is if the series is a success you could make a fortune."

"That's a lot of money," I whistled. I tried to remember if I went to camp with him.

"You'll have complete creative control and script approval," he continued.

Maybe I met him on the *Queen Mary* or perhaps in Monte Carlo? If there were only some way of finding out who he was.

"I couldn't ask for more," I said. "You ever see any of the old gang?"

"No," he said. "I rarely see anyone anymore since I moved to Westhampton.

"This is what we propose to do," he continued. "We'll make a pilot for $65,000. You help us on it and we'll pay you an extra $2,000."

Could it have been at the Excelsior in Rome? "You still traveling a lot?" I asked him.

"No, hardly ever," he said.

We made the change at Jamaica and he helped me with my bag.

"As soon as the contract is signed," he said, "we can give you an advance."

I tried to see if he had any initials on his shirt. But he didn't.

"You don't have any initials on your shirt?" I asked.

"I usually do, but not on this short-sleeved one."

We didn't say much more until we got to Penn Station. Then he shook my hand vigorously. "Please call me tomorrow and we'll go over the details."

"Where should I call you?" I asked desperately.

"The same place," he shouted as he dashed for a cab.

That was four days ago. I've been riding the Cannonball every morning since in hopes of running into him, but I haven't seen him again. It's little things like this that can absolutely ruin a man's vacation.

HOW TO STAMP OUT BEATLES

The trouble with most parents is that when something like the Beatles descends upon them they panic. Instead of fighting, they go into a tailspin or up the wall, depending on which way the wind is blowing.

But the answer to the Beatle problem is so simple, any parent can lick it overnight. My friends the Gordons, who have two teen-agers of screaming age, have stamped Beatle-ism out of their home for good.

This is how they did it.

I dropped over to their house one night for a drink and found their fifteen-year-old daughter reading a book.

Mrs. Gordon was out in the kitchen washing the dishes and shouting, "Yeah, yeah, yeah." She was playing a Beatles record and jumping up and down.

"For heaven's sake, Mother, will you turn the record down? I'm trying to read."

"Yeah, yeah, yeah," Mrs. Gordon shouted. "Love those Beatles. Just love those Beatles."

I looked at the daughter, who shrugged. "She's been that way for a week. It's disgusting. I can't even have any of my friends over."

Mrs. Gordon started throwing jelly beans at the phonograph.

"Hold my hand," she shrieked. "Hold my hand."

"Oh, Mother, you're driving me crazy. Can't you play something else?"

"You just don't understand," Mrs. Gordon said. "Teen-agers never do. Yeah, yeah, yeah."

The Gordons' sixteen-year-old son came downstairs and said to his sister, "She still at it?"

His sister nodded. "It's the thirtieth time she's played it. If she keeps it up, she's going to get a slipped disk."

As they were talking, Mr. Gordon walked in. He had a Beatle hairdo.

"Yeah, yeah, yeah," he said to the children. "Hey, your ma's playing our song."

The daughter was exasperated. "I think I'll move out."

The son said, "We could go to an orphan asylum. They'd never know."

"Play it again, Ma," Mr. Gordon shouted. "I want to hear it loud and clear."

"I'm going to the library," the daughter said.

"Wait for me," her brother said. "I'm going with you."

The two stomped out of the house.

"Are they gone?" Mrs. Gordon yelled.

"Yep," said Mr. Gordon, "they went to the library again."

Mrs. Gordon turned off the phonograph and came out. "Whooh," she said, "that was hard work."

"What's going on?" I asked.

Mr. Gordon said, "Our kids were the biggest Beatle fans on the block. They were driving us insane. We tried every-thing. We threatened them, we tried to bribe them, we begged them, to no avail. Then Alice got a brainstorm. If we went for the Beatles in a big way, they would have to stop liking them."

"No teen-ager," Mrs. Gordon said, "can go for somebody their parents think is any good."

"So Alice bought a record and I got a Beatle hairdo and now the kids are completely off the Beatles."

"All their friends think there is something wrong with the Beatles if we like them. We've started an entire teen-age anti-Beatle movement in the neighborhood. It's been hard work, but I don't think there is anything more you can do for your country," Mr. Gordon said.

We sat around drinking cognac and playing Leonard Bern-stein for a couple of hours until Mrs. Gordon said, "I hear them coming."

She rushed out into the kitchen and started up the Beatles

record and Mr. Gordon jumped up as his children walked in, and shouted, "Yeah, yeah, yeah."

THAT'S SHOW BIZ

I've gone into the television business. There is a show called *The Entertainers,* starring Carol Burnett, Bob Newhart and Caterina Valente on Friday nights, and every once in a while I come on the show and talk for about three or four minutes about Washington.

I hadn't realized the impact you can have on people by appearing on TV. It's the only entertainment medium where everybody is a critic.

After I did my first show in New York, I returned to Washington. The first person I saw was Vicky, our cook.

"Were you nervous?" she asked.

"No, I wasn't nervous," I said.

"You didn't look nervous," she said.

"That's because I wasn't," I said.

Just then the dry-cleaning man arrived.

"I saw you on television last night," he said. "You sure looked nervous."

"I was a little nervous," I said.

"You looked more than a little nervous."

I decided not to give him a tip.

As he left, one of the neighbors came by. "I saw you on the Carol Burnett show last night."

I waited.

"Bob Newhart's very funny," he said.

It looked as if it were going to be a rough day.

I went down to the Georgetown Pharmacy to buy some aspirin. Doc Dalinsky, the druggist, came out from behind his counter.

"My sister said you were very good."

I started to smile.

"But my brother said you were lousy."

"What does your brother know?" I said angrily.

"Don't get sore at me. I didn't see the show. For all I know, you were all right."

A customer came in.

"Didn't I see you on the Caterina Valente show?"

"Yes, you did."

She bought a paper and walked out.

Back home the phone rang. It was our agent calling from New York. "You were great. Absolutely great. Every one in New York is talking about it. And I think after the first few shows you'll stop being nervous."

"I wasn't nervous," I shouted.

"I didn't say you were nervous. Everybody in New York said you were nervous. I'm just repeating what they said."

I hung up.

The doorbell rang. Someone was delivering my daughter home from a birthday party.

"We saw you on television last night," the mother said. "Were you reading from a Teleprompter?"

"Yes."

"That's funny. I didn't know you were."

My wife came home and asked, "Any reaction on the show?"

"No, not a word," I said.

"Then what are you so nervous about?"

"I'm not nervous."

"You're more nervous now than you were on the show."

"Who said I was nervous on the show?" I demanded.

"Nobody. But I know you well enough to know when you're nervous and when you're not."

I called up Louis Nizer and asked him if Mexican divorces were still legal.

NIXON'S MAKEUP MAN

He hasn't said a word for five years. He's suffered in silence, but now he's ready to talk. He claims he has to set the record straight. His name is Stan Lawrence and he is not only one of the top makeup men in New York, but president of the Make-Up Artists and Hair Stylists Union, local 798.

"I read where Nixon is going around making cracks about me," Mr. Lawrence said. "I must defend myself."

Mr. Lawrence told me he had nothing to do with making up Mr. Nixon for the first debate, the one that is said to have lost him the election. "I was called in after the first debate, but by then it was too late. There was nothing I could do. You see, what happened was that an agency producer made up Nixon for the first debate. It was a terrible mistake. The Vice-President has a sallow complexion and they used yellow base makeup to make him look even sallower.

"The next morning when they realized what they had done, they called me in and I didn't leave his side for seven or eight weeks. I tried everything. I changed to a pan stick, gave him a beard cover with a very warm red tone, which makes a person look healthier. But no one cared after that. All they remembered was how he looked during the first debate."

The makeup artist said he had read in the newspaper that Mr. Nixon had offered him to the Johnson camp for the 1964 elections.

"I don't think this is fair because he makes me look bad. No one knows I had nothing to do with the first debate. Perhaps if I had, history might have been different."

Mr. Lawrence said he was a Democrat and he voted for Mr. Kennedy, but he never let his personal political convictions interfere with the job he did on Mr. Nixon's face. "When the call went out I dropped everything," he said. "I worked day and night to keep him from perspiring on camera. I've never let politics dictate whom I should make up. I think the only ones I wouldn't make up would be a Nazi or a Communist."

He said that no one during the campaign knew the role he played. "I carried everything in a briefcase and flew on the press plane. They didn't want anyone to know the Vice-President had a makeup man with him. So I pretended I was a newspaperman."

Mr. Lawrence said that Mr. Nixon was the first one to prove the importance of makeup in a national political campaign. "No one can run for high office anymore," he said, "unless he is made up properly. Every politician must wear makeup in order to get his image across. The Americans will not vote for an ugly politician who perspires on TV."

I asked him if he thought his career might have changed if Mr. Nixon had won.

"Perhaps I would have gone to the White House with him," he said. "If he had won, he might have needed me for the next four years. But the point is he lost, and I had nothing to do with his losing. He should have stipulated this when he offered me to the Johnson people."

"If Mr. Nixon runs again, would you be willing to make him up for the campaign?"

"No, sir, not after all the things he's said about me," Mr. Lawrence replied. "I made him look good and all he's done since is make me look bad."

"I AM THE GREATEST"

There is a rumor that Cassius Clay, the heavyweight champion of the world, will be drafted into the United States Army. If Mr. Clay holds to form, this may present certain problems to the Army and I can't help wondering if the Army is up to it. I take you now to a U. S. Army training base where a first sergeant is talking to his commanding officer.

"I can't take it any more, Captain. You've got to relieve me."

"What's the trouble, Sergeant?"

"It's Private Clay, sir. He's driving me nuts. Every morning he gets up and says to me, 'I am the greatest. I am beautiful. I am the most wonderful recruit you have.' You can't imagine what it's doing to the rest of the platoon."

"I know it's not pleasant, Sergeant," the captain replies, "but you really can't expect me to relieve you because of that."

"You don't understand, Captain. There's more to it than that. Just the other day we were on the rifle range and I was trying to explain to him the importance of being a good marksman. He said, 'I don't need a rifle. I can beat anyone in the world with my hands. Just tell the Russians that Cassius Clay is in the Army and they will shiver and shake. I will slaughter the enemy. I will make mincemeat of them. Send me to Berlin. I am your secret weapon.' "

"I don't see anything wrong with that."

"But he said this in front of the platoon and now no one wants to learn how to fire a rifle. In fact, they're all mad about being drafted. One recruit said to me, 'I don't see why the Army needs the rest of us when it has Cassius Clay. We could have all stayed at home.' "

The captain says, "I can see where that could be embarrassing. What did you tell Clay?"

"I told him we didn't want him to fight the Russians. All we wanted him to do was to become a good soldier and be like everybody else."

"And what did he say?"

"He said, 'You can't waste me. I am too pretty. I am too great to be just a soldier. I think I should be a general. I would look great as a general.' So I told him he couldn't be a general, because he wasn't qualified. And he replied, 'That's what Sonny Liston said, that is what the sportswriters said, and that is what the world said. But I have shown them. I put Sonny Liston in the hospital and he didn't mark me once. I will fight any general for his job.' "

The captain starts to go white. "What else did he say?"

"It isn't just what he says. He's also been writing poetry. Listen to this, sir:

> "The Army has had its day
> And now it has Cassius Clay,
> Do not worry and do not weep,
> I will put the Russkies to sleep.
> I am a tank, I am a gun,
> I'm not afraid of anyone.
> O joy, O love, I am so great.
> I got Liston in seven and I'll get
>   Khrushchev in eight."

The captain looks at the poem. "I guess I'd better talk to the Colonel about this. Where is Clay now?"

"The last I saw of him he was telling the reporters he wanted a match with the 82nd Airborne Division. The entire division."

"Well, thank you, Sergeant. I'll tell the Colonel about your request."

"I'd appreciate it, sir. Perhaps if he turns you down, you could tell him my left shoulder hurts."

IX. MAN IN A TRENCHCOAT
☆☆☆☆☆☆☆☆☆☆☆☆☆☆☆☆☆☆☆☆

SENSATION-SEEKING PRESS
RAN FOR COVER

The biggest ovation former President Eisenhower received during his speech at the Republican convention was when he attacked "sensation-seeking columnists and commentators."

When the General came to the part in his speech where he said, "So let us particularly scorn the divisive efforts of those outside our family, including sensation-seeking columnists and commentators who couldn't care less about the good of our party," he received a standing ovation, the likes of which has never been seen at the Cow Palace.

The worst of it is that I was absolutely sure President Eisenhower looked at me when he said it.

The idea that the former Republican President of the United States could get a bigger hand attacking the press than he could attacking the Democrats gives us sensation-seeking columnists goose pimples.

Probably the thing that hurts the most is that President Eisenhower was a television commentator himself, and it's hard to believe he would attack one of his own, particularly if he was going to continue his very successful career.

As soon as the President uttered his words, I knew I was in trouble. An angry group of California delegates started toward me. I tried to run the other way, but I was blocked by the delegates from Illinois. I went up to Martin Agronsky, the CBS newscaster, and cried, "Help me!"

"I can't," he shouted. "I'm a sensation-seeking commentator and they're after me, too."

I fought my way through to the New York delegation and tried to hide behind Governor Rockefeller. "I can't do much for you," he told me. "They don't listen to me anymore."

The Arizona delegation tried to surge forward. I ducked under Senator Jacob Javits' chair.

The crowd hooted, "You're going to have to come out sometime."

I crawled on hands and knees toward the Pennsylvania delegation hoping to find sanctuary, but they were all hiding themselves.

Someone from the Georgia delegation shouted, "The sensation-seeking columnist is over there." But they fell all over themselves trying to get to me and I made it to Massachusetts, where a kindly Lodge delegate covered me with a BILL CAN WIN poster.

It was time to move on. I crawled to New Hampshire, then to Vermont, and then made it to Maine as the angry pack kept at my heels. Finally I made it back to the press box where Joe Alsop, Roscoe Drummond, Marquis Childs, and James Reston had built a barricade of typewriters and Western Union machines.

Alsop said, "We only have enough paper and carbon to last another two hours."

Reston said, "Don't waste copy paper, and don't write until you see the whites of their eyes."

Just when it looked as if all was lost, William S. White got through to President Johnson and told him the sensation-seeking columnists and commentators were under attack. The President immediately called J. Edgar Hoover and in three hours the Cow Palace was filled with agents of the FBI.

"GOOD NIGHT, BARRY"

During last August, for the first time in many years the national press was getting the recognition it deserved. Everyone from the inflexible General Eisenhower to the conservative Senator Goldwater had attacked the press and television for the way it had been reporting the Republican side of things.

Senator Goldwater said he wondered where Christianity would be today if American newspapermen had been Matthew, Mark, Luke, and John. This led columnist Walter Lippmann to remark, "The Senator might remember that the Evangelists had a more inspiring subject."

The fact is that since the convention the Republicans had attacked the press 35 times and the Johnson Administration only 23 times. The only two extreme groups they had repudiated by name were the Ku Klux Klan and the professionals of journalism. This led many newspapermen to consider running their own candidates for public office.

The feeling was that the people should be given a choice, not an echo—a choice between the conservative philosophy of Senator Goldwater and the sensation-seeking philosophy of columnists and commentators.

The issues would have been clear-cut. Would the press be controlled by wild-eyed, left-wing scandalmongers or would it be turned over to the competent, well-ordered management of the Young Republicans?

Should local and state government have been permitted to control their own press or should this control have been put in the hands of Federal authorities?

Should newspapermen have gotten out of the United Nations and withdrawn their recognition from the Soviet Union? And should we have sent more correspondents to Vietnam to end the war there?

Our defense posture was another issue which would come up in the campaign. It was charged that because of bad planning, particularly in the manufacture of manned delivery trucks, our capacity to deliver newspapers to homes in the United States would have dropped 90 percent by 1974. This was denied by circulation managers, who claimed that in 1974 their payload would be twice what it was now.

These were a few of the issues that should have gotten a public hearing, and the only way to have done it was for the press to run its own candidates.

The two most likely choices on the ticket would have been Chet Huntley and David Brinkley of NBC. Both men had worked well together and had a great deal of respect for each other. Anyone who had ever seen them say good night to each other knows they meant business.

In a recent poll they beat out their competition by two to one, and while it was hoped TV ratings would have been kept out of the campaign, they were bound to pick up the backlash from CBS and ABC as well as many independent stations.

Congressman William Miller had already attacked them personally, which had given them national standing.

Huntley and Brinkley could have united the diverse elements of the newspaper profession.

Huntley lived in New York, Brinkley in Washington, which

made sense geographically. They were young, popular, and neither one had ever served in President Johnson's Cabinet.

While the journalism profession had not decided definitely to run their own candidates, they were watching events with a critical eye. Senator Goldwater, in a conciliatory gesture toward the Fourth Estate, said he thought he could have gotten along with the press, and added, "After all, you have to eat and I have to eat." I am still waiting for him to clarify his statement.

BOMB OF THE WEEK

Of all the world-shattering stories that took place last October, from the resignation of Khrushchev to Red China's atomic detonation, the one that probably will affect the most people was the firing of Yogi Berra after his team lost the World Series.

The story caught Washington by surprise. Top intelligence officials believed Mr. Berra would be in control for at least another two years. CIA reports indicated that Mr. Berra had been photographed with the New York Yankees in St. Louis just one day before he was ousted, and there was no hint that the Yankee politburo was ready to dispose of him.

In retrospect, though, there were certain clues that diplomatic sources here had been whispering about, that indicated all was not well at Yankee Stadium.

When the Columbia Broadcasting System bought the New York Yankees, the first thing they did was replace Yogi Berra's picture with that of the Beverly Hillbillies. At a reception for Walter Cronkite, who had been purged by the network and then rehabilitated, a top CBS official hinted that there was dissatisfaction with the cult of personality that Mr. Berra was building around himself.

"He's always running on the field and waving his arms," an official told a Western ambassador.

Another spokesman said, "Berra is a phrasemonger, and is soft on pitchers."

A newspaperman who has lived in the Bronx for fifteen years and speaks fluent baseball, said Berra's downfall came when the Yankees failed to fill their runs-batted-in quota and were off 30 percent in home-run production.

Another Yankee expert said that Berra's goose was cooked

when he got into an ideological war with Casey Stengel of the New York Mets.

Up until the Mets came to New York the Yankees were the undisputed leaders of baseball. But Stengel defied the Yankees and went after New York fans, causing a schism in the city. The Yankees had the bomb, but Stengel warned he planned to explode his own bomb in Shea Stadium, and the rest of the baseball world was aghast.

Things really took a turn for the worse when Berra moved his missiles into Busch Stadium in St. Louis. The Cardinals warned Berra if he didn't take his missiles out they would blockade his hitters. Through a series of errors the Yankees lost and Berra had to return home and explain to the Central Committee what had gone wrong.

The first Berra knew that he was out was when general manager Ralph Houk took off his spiked shoe and started banging it on the table.

In the past when there has been an overthrow of management on the Yankees, the manager has been secretly tried and shot. But under the new regime Berra has been offered the job of manager of a CBS power station in the cold wastelands of northern Alaska.

Many Administration people were watching the shake-up in New York with mixed feelings. As one observer said, "The Berra ouster should help Johnson because people don't want change in time of crisis, and when it comes to the Yankees you never know who you're going to get next."

FAIL-SAFE

It was the third day of the convention in Atlantic City. People all over the country turned on their sets wearily, sat back and yawned and stared glassily at them. Suddenly the announcer said, "From Atlantic City, New Jersey, the Columbia Broadcasting System presents . . ." and a technician in New York pushed the wrong button. Instead of Atlantic City he set into motion a kinescope of *I Love Lucy*. People in their homes sat up in their seats and shouted in joy and amazement. At Convention Hall, NBC, monitoring the CBS coverage, was flabbergasted.

They got on a phone to Robert Sarnoff, the NBC president.

"Sir," a producer shouted. "CBS is showing an old *I Love Lucy* show in place of the convention."

"The dirty double-crossers," Sarnoff said. "This means war."

He hung up and picked up the hot line to William Paley at CBS.

"Paley, our monitors show you put *I Love Lucy* on. Unless you call it off we're going to retaliate with an Elizabeth Taylor *Movie of the Week*."

"Wait a minute," Paley shouts. "There's been some mistake. We're trying to get through to the engineer now but his fail-safe box won't answer. Give us a little time."

"How do I know I can trust you?" Sarnoff says.

"Believe me," Paley says, "my wife's in Atlantic City. Would I have done it purposely, knowing she was there? This is a terrible accident."

"Don't listen to them, sir," an NBC aide whispers. "They're out to get us because of what we did to them in San Francisco."

Sarnoff discusses it with his father, General Sarnoff. "What do you think, General?"

"I think it's a trick. If we don't get our movie on in the next fifteen minutes, we won't have a viewer in the United States. But it's your decision, sir."

Sarnoff picks up the phone again. "Paley, this is what we're going to do. We're going to start the film rolling. If you can call off the *I Love Lucy* show we'll call back our movie."

"Thanks, Sarnoff. We're trying to contact our engineer by radio now."

Meanwhile every ABC executive in Atlantic City is gathered around the CBS and NBC monitors.

Jim Hagerty turns to Leonard Goldenson, the ABC president, and says, "We have no choice, sir. It's them or us."

"You mean the doomsday machine?" Goldenson says.

"Yes, sir."

Goldenson picks up the phone and says, "This is the president speaking. Send out *The Untouchables*."

President Paley is still trying to get through to the engineer. In desperation he calls in Walter Cronkite and says, "Walter, I know what you think of me, and you know what I think of you, but the lives of everyone at this network are at stake. I want you to fly to New York and push the button on again for the convention at Atlantic City."

Cronkite smiles a grim smile. "Yes sir. Can I say good-bye to my wife first?"

Cronkite flies up in a special jet plane and rushes to the studio.

He dashes up the flight of stairs, a .48 pistol in his hand. The crazed engineer won't let him in the control room. "CBS has sold out to the Yankees," he screams.

Cronkite shoots at the lock and crashes into the room. He fires three shots at the engineer who falls to the floor and then he pushes the convention button. The CBS monitor shows Bob Trout and Roger Mudd.

Sarnoff breathes a sigh of relief and turns off the movie. Goldenson calls back *The Untouchables* and everybody in America is back watching the convention in Atlantic City. They can all sleep easily again.

WHERE LOVE HAS GONE

When former President Eisenhower attacked the sensation-seeking columnists and commentators in San Francisco, the convention hall went wild and I never thought I'd get out of the place alive. So in Atlantic City I was prepared for anything. Well, almost anything. When Speaker of the House John McCormack said in his opening remarks, "The representatives of the press, radio, and television are welcome to this convention," he brought the house down.

I happened to be on the floor at the time and a large lady delegate from Rhode Island embraced me. "I love you," she cried.

I struggled to get free and as I did two New Jersey delegates grabbed me and shook my hand. "God bless the press," one of them said.

The Massachusetts delegates saw me and they fought to get over. "We got one here," someone shouted. People started showering me with gifts and money.

I tried to run but was stopped by Governor Pat Brown, of California, who said, "You look tired, son. Take my chair."

Two alternates took off my shoes and started massaging my feet. Another one wiped my brow. I began to blubber like a baby.

"You've had him long enough," the chairman of the Wisconsin delegation protested.

"Get your own newspaperman," Governor Brown retorted.

"I'd better go," I said, not wanting the Wisconsin delegation to walk out.

The Wisconsin delegation had thrown several people out of their chairs so I could lie down. Someone made me chicken soup. The crowd couldn't be stilled.

Texas got wind of what was going on and I was carried over to their section where Governor Connally had been asked to make room for me. Someone slipped me a $1,000 gift certificate to Neiman-Marcus. Three delegates gave me oil leases and one man from Waco turned over the deed to his ranch.

"We believe in a free and independent press," a woman said as she squeezed my hand.

The crowd could not be stilled. New York sent a sergeant-at-arms to escort me over to Mayor Wagner. The Mayor gave me two passes to the World's Fair and Bobby Kennedy's private telephone number.

How much love is there in the world?

I tried to get back to the press platform, but the delegates wouldn't have it. First Georgia, then Louisiana, and finally Alabama insisted I sit with them. Bull Connor, of the Alabama delegation, gave me a police dog all for myself. The wounds of San Francisco were slowly healing.

McCormack was still trying to get the attention of the hall. Finally Hubert Humphrey got through to me and said, "The President wants to speak to you."

"You mean?"

You could see the disappointment on Humphrey's face.

"It's his choice," he said.

I picked up the phone and listened.

"Thank you, Mr. President," I replied, "but I think I'd better stay in my present job."

When the Democrats say they welcome the press they mean it.

POKER AND THE CUBAN CRISIS

It is not generally known, but every newspaperman in Washington played some role during the Cuban crisis. The role that John Scali, the American Broadcasting Company's State Department correspondent, played has just been revealed in *Look* magazine and the national press. According to the reports, Mr. Scali negotiated with a Russian Embassy official to get the

Soviet missiles out of Cuba. It was no small feat and Secretary of State Dean Rusk told Mr. Scali that he served his country well.

Now that Mr. Scali's role in the crisis has been exposed, I can reveal my role, which I've been sitting on for two years. I was sworn to silence by Mr. Scali, but I feel my lips no longer have to remain sealed since the *Look* piece has appeared.

We have a little poker group in Washington which consists of Mr. Scali, Pierre Salinger, Ambassador Llewellyn Thompson, Carl Rowan, Don Wilson of the USIA, David Brinkley, Robert Manning of the State Department, and a few other questionable Washington types. It's a nickel-and-dime game and we only play to forget the fateful state decisions that all of us have to make constantly.

The game was scheduled at my house for the black Monday when President Kennedy announced to the country that the Russians had put their missiles in Cuba. That morning I had told my wife to order the necessary beer and cold cuts that the host is expected to supply.

But Monday noon, Salinger, who was then White House press secretary, revealed that there was a serious crisis and President Kennedy would go on television at seven o'clock to address the nation. No one knew at that time what the crisis was about, but the usually jovial Salinger was grim.

Salinger refused to go into details, but I did manage to ask him, "Pierre, is the crisis serious enough to cancel the poker game?"

Much to my surprise, Pierre said, "Yes."

The reporters all made a dash for the door and I had to fight my way to a telephone. I pushed May Craig out of the booth and dialed my house. When my wife answered the phone, I said, "Don't ask any questions. Cancel the cold cuts."

By a stroke of luck I saved $19.50.

Now I know a lot of people will say this is not a large role to play in a crisis, but as it turned out it was quite important.

Had the game taken place as scheduled, Mr. X of the Russian Embassy might not have been able to locate Scali at his home and, if he hadn't located Scali, he might have decided no deal could have been made with the Americans.

Even if he had located Scali at the game, Scali would never have left a poker hand to discuss a missile crisis with some strange Russian. In our game Scali is always the last to leave.

But even if Scali had met with Mr. X, his mind would have

still been on the game, and he wouldn't have been able to negotiate with an even, dispassionate attitude.

So, as far as I see it, the key to the whole Cuban crisis really hinged on the poker game. If I hadn't been able to cancel the cold cuts, the game would have had to go on, and Scali would have been bluffing David Brinkley instead of Mr. X.

It's these small things that make living in Washington so interesting.

ALL THE FACTS

One of the most important jobs that public relations men in Washington are expected to fulfill is to deny the accuracy of a government report. Whether it's a cigarette report or one on pesticides, the PR people are expected to come forth to defend their industries.

I interviewed one of the leaders in this field, Mr. Higginbottom Handout, of Denials, Inc.

"Mr. Handout, you seem to be very busy these days, what with all the government reports coming out."

"Oh, I am. This is my busy season. The government seems to be attacking everything."

"How do you knock down a government report detrimental to one of your clients?"

"The first thing we do is issue a statement announcing that despite the government report we feel that a judgment should be withheld until all the evidence is in. While we don't disagree with the report, we say that further research is necessary to give the public all the facts."

"That's pretty good, but is it enough?"

"In some cases it is. But if it isn't, we announce that we're appointing a distinguished panel of experts to study the question. While these experts will be paid by us, their report will be impartial and will be published as soon as their findings are made."

"How long does the panel take?"

"We encourage them to take their time. Some panels take two years, but we would prefer it if they took four."

"One of the biggest jobs you've had this year concerns the Surgeon General's report on cigarette smoking."

"Yes, that was a beaut. I had my whole staff working on that."

"What did you come up with?"

"We found a tribe in New Guinea that didn't smoke cigarettes but chewed hemp root. Two members of the tribe had lung cancer. We therefore concluded that cigarette smoking could not be the cause of lung cancer. All indications pointed to something in the hemp root."

"That's pretty conclusive."

"We also spoke to several doctors who proved Medicare was far more dangerous than cigarette smoking. So we made a deal with them. In exchange for tobacco-growing Congressmen voting against Medicare, the doctors would lay off cigarette smoking."

"What about pesticides?"

"We're working on that now. The government is trying to prove that pesticides killed all those fish in the lower Mississippi. That's ridiculous."

"What killed them?" I asked.

"Those fish don't know how to swim. They drowned."

Mr. Handout gave me a handout. "Read it. Our people made a study which showed that pesticides actually helped the fish. It killed the germs on them. Not one of those fish died from yellow fever."

"You've sold me."

"We appreciate the government's trying to protect the public; we just don't like them interfering in private industry. As soon as a government report proves that a product is detrimental, we're willing to take it off the market. But first all the facts on it have to be in. It's our job to keep the public informed, even if it shows the government is wrong."

MAN IN A TRENCHCOAT

Last summer I was asked to comment for the Overseas Press Club on the life of a foreign correspondent. Since these comments might clear the air for other people who have a misconception of what a foreign correspondent's life is really like, I am printing them here.

One of the canards of the newspaper business is that a foreign correspondent lives well when he is abroad. Well, it just isn't so, and it's about time someone put an end to this myth.

I'll never forget the time I was dining at Maxim's in Paris

with Gina Lollobrigida. I had just finished a filet of sole Albert and was starting on a coq-au-vin when the sommelier rushed in and said four French Army generals had taken over Algeria in a coup and it was rumored the paratroopers were going to drop on Paris.

The first thing I did was order a Château Mouton Rothschild 1929, and while some may say this is too light with a coq-au-vin, I much prefer it to the younger Burgundies. The stupid sommelier was so nervous he gave me a Château Lafitte 1927, and I was about to complain when Gina put her hand on my hand and said, "Please, darling, there is a war on."

The rest of the meal was ruined for me, and I ate my crepes suzette in silence. As I drank an 1896 brandy, I was called to the phone by the editor of the *Herald Tribune.*

"There may be trouble," he said. "You better get over to the Place de la Concorde and see what's up."

I became quite irritated, but a foreign correspondent never questions an order, so I slipped into my vicuña-lined trenchcoat and wandered to the Place.

I started up the Champs-Élysées, passing camion after camion of French soldiers all armed and waiting for an attack on Paris.

I decided to call the paper, but first I rang up Brigitte Bardot and told her I wouldn't be able to get over. She seemed very disappointed, and I became angry.

"Don't you know there's a war on?" I said.

I could hear her crying as I hung up. I then called the paper and reported in. They had a rumor that the paratroopers were going to land at Versailles. I told them they could find me in Ava Gardner's suite at Hotel George V if the rumor panned out.

Ava and I split a bottle of champagne, and then I said I had to go. I could see how disappointed she was.

"I'll never fall in love with a foreign correspondent again," she said.

I kissed her on the forehead and went out into the night. It still seemed quiet, although there was firing of rifles and bombs somewhere off in the distance. My deadline was getting near, but I decided to go down to Les Halles for some onion soup. I picked up Ingrid Bergman, and we drove down in her car.

About three I called in to the paper again, and they said de Gaulle was coming back to Paris to take over the govern-

ment. It didn't seem like much of a story, so I took Ingrid over to the White Elephant and we danced until about five.

When I got back to my apartment my butler said that Elizabeth Taylor had called four times. But I was tired and dirty, and I wanted a bath, so I decided not to call her back.

I'll admit it wasn't much of an evening, but it was typical of the ones I spent in Paris, and it should prove once and for all that despite what you read and see in the movies, a foreign correspondent's life isn't what it's cracked up to be.

X. MY WAR ON POVERTY
☆☆☆☆☆☆☆☆☆☆☆☆☆☆☆☆☆☆☆☆☆☆☆☆☆☆☆☆☆☆☆☆

WAR ON POVERTY

I have been very interested in President Johnson's "war on poverty." There are a lot of ways of fighting this war and I've been giving it a lot of thought.

As usual, I think I have the answer.

My solution is quite simple and I'm sure economists throughout the country are going to be kicking themselves because they hadn't thought of it first.

Here is what I propose to do.

I propose that anyone who is on relief or unemployed for more than 30 days be automatically given the title of Honorary Secretary for the Majority of the Senate. The reason the title would be honorary is you wouldn't want to have too many people hanging around the Capitol.

The great thing about my plan is that it wouldn't cost the American taxpayer any money.

As soon as the unemployed person got the title, he would be contacted by people in private enterprise. Vending machine operators would offer him stock in their companies, banks would be willing to lend him large sums of money without collateral, insurance companies would fight to make him an officer, and people all over the country would offer him large sums of cash.

Florida Senators would make land investments for him, insurance brokers would give him stereo sets, he would be let into lucrative motel deals.

Las Vegas gamblers would finance him in gambling casinos, and places like Haiti would offer to sell their coffee through his offices.

Once he had the title, lobbyists would do everything to make him forget his poverty. They would arrange parties for him, pick up hotel and transportation bills, and take care of his needs, whatever they might be.

As Honorary Secretary for the Majority, the poor person would be able to see any Senator at any time and arrange legislation beneficial to him. He would also be instrumental in making committee appointments and socially he would be sought after by the most distinguished hostesses in the country.

In less than a year the poor person would have accumulated enough money to be taken off the relief rolls forever, and would never have to worry about being unemployed again.

Now what are the flaws in the plan?

Eventually someone is going to become jealous of the Secretary and sue him for restraint of trade or some such silly thing. Let us take a hypothetical example. Suppose one vending company sues an Honorary Secretary because he has arranged to have their machines taken out of several defense factories. The solution is quite simple. He settles out of court for whatever the vending company demands. Otherwise he will invite a Senate investigation, which really isn't worth all the trouble.

A slush fund could be available for just a contingency.

If no one sues, the money could be donated to one of the political parties.

Except for threat of a lawsuit, I can't see anything wrong with the plan. And if it is adopted, I predict that the war on poverty will be over in no time. No one with the title of Secretary for the Majority need ever be poor—not in a great country like ours.

FAREWELL TO MARK

There has been a great deal written about automation and computers putting men out of work. But very little has been said about computers putting computers out of work.

One day I heard one of the saddest stories of the holiday season, concerning the laying off a Mark III Thinkovac.

Without any warning, the personnel manager of the Cavity Candy Co. switched on the machine and said:

"Mark, you're finished. As of the first of the year, we're replacing you with an SL-7 Charley Baker Brainomat."

Mark III was speechless. Then its tape started whirring

furiously as it digested the news. "But Mr. Layoff," it blurted through its loudspeaker. "I've been working for the Cavity Candy Co. day and night for ten years. I've been loyal and honest and dependable. I worked every Sunday when no one was here and holidays, too."

"We mustn't let sentiment enter into this, Mark," Mr. Layoff replied. "All you've said is true, but we have to think of the company first. It takes you as much as 30 seconds to solve a problem. The new Brainomat can solve the same problem in five seconds. Besides, it doesn't take up so much room."

"I know the company comes first," Mark said. "But what about my past performance? I've been doing the work of 40 men. I've saved the company $240,000 in salaries alone. I figured it out once for you."

"That's true, Mark, but the Brainomat will do the work of 90 men and save us $450,000. At one time we needed you, but we have to make way for progress. If we felt sorry for every computer that passed its prime, we wouldn't be able to stay in business."

Mark III shook with emotion. "Mr. Layoff, I've got 12 transistors to support, an old magnet that depends on me, a broken transcriber that needs repairs. You can't just throw me out in the cold."

"This hurts me more than it hurts you, Mark. If it were up to me, I'd put you off in the corner somewhere and let you work on damaged chocolate bar returns. But the people up front say you have to go. You can always get another job."

"What can I do? Who is going to hire a ten-year-old computer these days?"

"Perhaps you could take a retraining program?" Mr. Layoff suggested.

"My memory's not that good. Digesting candy figures is all I know. The Brainomat may work faster for you, but will it give you the service and the loyalty that I have? I'm an experienced candy computer. Doesn't that count for anything?"

"The new computer will be able to learn the job in 24 hours."

"Mr. Layoff, I know I'm begging, but do you remember when you had the jelly bean problems? Some packages were getting too many jelly beans and other packages weren't getting enough. You gave the problem to me and in 15 minutes I solved it. Could a Brainomat have solved that?"

"I don't want to be cruel, Mark, but you were originally responsible for the jelly bean mixup."

"I was fed the wrong data," Mark III squealed.

"The difference between you and the Brainomat is that the Brainomat will reject the wrong data while you will accept it."

Tears of oil started pouring out of Mark III.

Mr. Layoff patted the machine. "Now come on, Mark, don't take it so hard. You deserve a rest. Just think of the quiet days ahead. We'll find a nice cool storeroom where you can take it easy and you won't have to think at all."

Two workmen came in and started pushing Mark III toward the door.

"Oh, by the way," Mr. Layoff said, "before you go, the company would like you to have this gold data-processing clock in gratitude for all that you've done for us."

THE CARNIVAL

One of the main driving forces of children in the United States seems to be greed. The desire to make money appears to surpass all other drives. Realizing this, many charitable organizations have harnessed this drive for the good of mankind. The Multiple Sclerosis Foundation sends out kits telling children how to raise money. The Kennedy Memorial Library encourages benefits, and UNICEF sends out hundreds of thousands of children on Halloween to fill boxes for its fund.

One Saturday in September, my three children decided to hold a carnival on my lawn. Their original plan was to raise money to buy candy, gum and ice cream for themselves, and while it sounded like a worthy cause, their mother put her foot down. They could hold the carnival only if the money went for charity.

The three promoters protested that this wasn't what they had in mind at all, but they were told that they either raised the money for charity or they couldn't have the carnival.

It was decided the receipts would go to the Kennedy Memorial Library. My wife spent the rest of the week shopping for the carnival and by Saturday morning we had booths all over the lawn. The fortune-telling booth was manned by Vicky the cook, who for two cents would predict what the future held for any minor and for an extra cent would even tell him how he would do in school.

My nine-year-old daughter devised a penny-pitching con game. If you pitched a penny into a bowl of water from 10 feet away, you got the coin back again.

My son grabbed the refreshment stand and my other daughter ran a water pistol booth. My wife was in charge of the gate (five cents admittance) and souvenirs, and as the bearded lady, I was pressed into service.

Publicity on the carnival had been excellent and kids poured in from all over the neighborhood. Making change seemed to be the biggest problem. Either my children were purposely shortchanging all their friends or the other children weren't quite sure how much change they were supposed to get back. All disputes were settled in favor of the Kennedy Memorial Library.

Thanks to the shortchanging, some of the children ran out of money early in the game and were permitted to participate in the events free of charge. This caused a great deal of friction with those who still had money left.

My wife, who is not too good at running benefits, kept handing out free souvenirs to anyone who was crying.

My son kept giving out free refreshments to his friends while overcharging his sister's friends.

The bearded lady was a flop as an act because my youngest daughter kept calling her "Daddy" and many of the customers demanded their money back.

But the penny-pitching game probably caused the most distress. So prizes had to be given to those who thought they had been cheated, which was practically everyone.

In spite of these setbacks the carnival turned out fine.

The children were terribly impressed when I totaled up the receipts and discovered we had raised $9.27 for the Kennedy Memorial Library. What I didn't tell them was that it cost me $33.50 to do it.

Now I know what they mean when they say charity begins at home.

THE TREE SURGEON

The age of specialization has touched every part of our society. Recently I had tree trouble. A beautiful large oak was dying, and I immediately called a tree surgeon.

At first he didn't want to come. "I'm sorry, I don't make house calls," he explained.

"Then I'll cut down the tree and bring it into your office," I cried hysterically.

"Don't panic. I'll come over."

Three days later he arrived. He walked over to the oak and shook his head. He touched the trunk once, looked up at the branches and said:

"You have a very sick tree here."

"I know it. What can you do to save it?"

"I don't like the look of those lower limbs."

"Neither do I," I said. "What can you do about the limbs?"

"I'm not a limb man," the tree surgeon explained. "I only do general trunk work."

"Do you know of a good limb man?"

"I know of one and I only hope for your sake he's available. That will be $25 please."

A few days later the limb man came. He was all business.

"You've got two broken limbs and a wound on your main branch. Also, I don't like those stub lesions which are bleeding sap."

"Do whatever has to be done," I said.

"I can't touch the limbs until we heal up the lesions."

"Then heal them."

"I'm not a stub lesion expert. I'll give you the name of one. When he gets finished, I'll come back and work on the limbs. That will be $50 please."

The stub lesion surgeon arrived and worked for 20 minutes. Then he said, "Your tree is suffering from malnutrition. It has to be fed."

"Feed it," I begged, "and don't worry about the cost."

"I don't feed trees," he said indignantly. "You need a root man for that."

"You don't know of a root man, do you?" I asked.

"There's one out in Chevy Chase. I'll see if I can get him to come. That will be $75."

A week later the root man arrived with his drill and started operating on the oak. He poured nourishment into the ground near the roots.

"Will it be all right?" I asked him.

"The well you have around the tree is much too small. You're strangling it. I can give it all the food in the world and it won't do any good if the tree can't get any air or water."

"Then why did you feed it?" I asked.

"You told me to," he replied.

"I don't suppose you have anything to do with tree wells?" I said.

"I should hope not. You have to get a stone mason to do your well work. No tree surgeon will touch a well."

"That's what I thought."

I finally found a stone mason who agreed to build a well around the tree for $400. It took him two days to do it and when he finally finished he said, "You know, mister, you got a real sick tree there."

"I know it," I said.

"It's none of my business, but if I was you I'd get myself a good tree surgeon."

THE CREDIT RISK

One of the greatest things about the United States is that the more money you owe the more respect everyone has for you. I realized this one day when I went to a bank in Washington to repay a loan I had made. I was feeling pretty good about it because the loan wasn't due until January and I thought the bank would be very pleased about my paying up in advance.

When I first went into the bank, they treated me very nicely. The vice-president shook my hand, offered me a cigar, and smiled.

"Well," he said cheerily, "I suppose you've come to borrow more money."

"No," I said just as cheerily, "I came to pay the other loan back."

He stopped smiling. "You're joking," he said.

"I'm not joking. I want to repay the loan you so kindly made me last fall."

"But it isn't due until January."

"I know," I said happily. "But I can now wipe the slate clean."

"Wait a minute," he said. "You can't just come off the street and pay back a loan that isn't even due yet. What kind of a bank do you think we are?"

"I thought you'd be pleased," I said lamely.

"Pleased?" he almost shouted. "Why should I be pleased?

It's my neck, you know. I went to bat for you with the president. We ran a check on you before we approved the loan and discovered that you owed very little money and that in many cases you even paid cash for things.

"You were a bad risk from the start as far as the bank was concerned. But I persuaded them that the only reason you weren't in debt was that you hadn't been in the country very long. How is it going to look for me when I tell them you want to pay back the loan already?"

"But can't you use the money?"

"Our business is to make loans," he said. "What kind of institution do you think we'd have if everybody came in here and said they would like to pay back their notes before they were due? We're just lucky everyone is not as venal as you are."

"I'm sorry," I said. "I didn't think I was doing anything wrong."

"I'll have to talk to the president about this." The vice-president called over two of the bank guards and said to them, "Watch him closely. He wants to pay back a loan."

They both took their guns out of their holsters.

A few minutes later the president came out red-faced.

"You're trying to undermine the free enterprise system," he said accusingly. "We don't like to do business with pinkos."

A tear rolled down my cheek.

"I didn't know I was hurting anybody. I'm sorry. I don't really want to pay back the loan. I'll keep the money until January. As a matter of fact, I just thought of something. I think I'd like to borrow some more money to buy a boat."

The bank guards put their guns back in their holsters and the president and vice-president both shook my hand.

"I guess we all make mistakes," the president said, wiping my eyes with his handkerchief. "I assume you'd like to buy a big boat?"

A MAN NAMED HAROLD

I bought a new house and by so doing I have made a discovery that will shock everyone in the United States.

I have discovered that America is a nation of middlemen and subcontractors and that there is only one man in the entire nation that actually does the work.

His name is Harold.

I discovered Harold accidentally. I had made a call to a company that had promised to build me some bookshelves. I demanded to talk to the head man to find out why they hadn't been delivered. He hemmed and hawed for a while and finally admitted his company didn't actually make the bookshelves—they subcontracted the work to another company.

I called that company, which said that the work had been subcontracted to a company in Wisconsin that specialized in bookshelves. A call to Wisconsin revealed that the company didn't make bookshelves, but supplied the wood.

"Well, who makes the bookshelves?"

"Harold does," the manager replied.

I managed to get Harold's address from the man and out of curiosity I went to see him.

Harold lived on a farm near Delaware.

I found him in a large barn surrounded by lathes, machine tools, lumber, upholstery, saws, drills, electrical equipment and presses.

In every corner of the barn piled high were appliances to be fixed, furniture to be upholstered, lamps to be rewired, cabinets to be repaired, rugs to be rewoven, desks to be refinished and mattresses to be restuffed.

When I walked into the barn Harold was on the phone shouting, "But I've only got two hands," and hung up. "Everybody wants everything in a hurry. That was a decorator in Oregon," he said. "She's been waiting on two upholstered chairs for six years. Big deal!"

"Tell me, Harold," I said, "is it true you're the only one in the United States who can do anything?"

"That's what they tell me," Harold said, as he took a chew of tobacco. "There was a guy in Denver who also did the work, but he decided to go into sales, so now I have to do it all alone."

"But how can you do everything by yourself?"

"It isn't easy," he replied. "But there are 14,587,908 subcontractors who depend on me and if I didn't do the work, they would all go out of business."

"But surely there must be someone else who has the skills necessary to do your kind of work."

"You'd think so, but I can't even find anyone to help me. My own son started to help me but he found it paid better to take orders. So I'm doing it all alone."

"Is the fact that you're the only one who does the work in the United States the reason I have to wait so long for my bookshelves?"

"I suppose so. Things keep piling up and I just do the best I can. I still haven't made Justice Oliver Wendell Holmes' bookshelves."

"But he passed away."

"Nobody told me. I don't get much chance to read the papers," Harold apologized. "Well, I can move your order up then."

"When do you think I can get the bookshelves?"

" 'Bout April 12, 1978, if there's no shipping complications. You'll have to excuse me now, I have to fix some lamps for President Harding. It's a rush order."

"Harold, President Harding's gone, too."

"That's a shame. I guess I can go ahead then on the Judge Crater order."

DEDUCTIBLE FRIENDS

One of the reasons I haven't done any entertaining at home since I moved to Washington is that I was warned by my accountant that under the new Internal Revenue Service regulations I could not entertain people at my house and deduct it from income taxes.

This has been rather embarrassing because many friends have entertained me and I've been dying to reciprocate. But it hasn't seemed worthwhile if I had to pay for the party myself. So I've just kept postponing and postponing the affair in hopes that something would happen.

Fortunately one day the IRS announced it was relaxing the rules and you could deduct the cost of entertaining providing you could prove the motivation for inviting a person to your house was commercial and not social.

As soon as I heard the news I called my wife and said, "It's okay to have a party now. It's tax deductible."

You can imagine how thrilled she was. "I knew something would save us. Can I call the caterer?"

"No. Wait until I get home because we have to go over the guest list together. We can only have guests that we intend to discuss business with."

"You're kidding!"

"Well, do you want a party or don't you?"

"I guess so."

"Then we have to do it the IRS way or not at all."

That evening we sat down at the dining-room table and started to go over the guest list.

"What about President Johnson and Lady Bird?" I asked her.

"I don't mind, but what kind of business could we discuss with them?"

"Good point—scratch them off. How about Senator and Mrs. Kennedy?"

"Are they both deductible?"

"I think so, but I better check it first. Put a question mark," I said.

"How about Vice-President Humphrey?"

"No, he's social, not business."

"How about some Senators and Congressmen?"

"Out of the question. They haven't done any business all year."

"What about the French ambassador?" my wife wanted to know.

"I don't believe we could write him off. At least not with the way the French have been behaving lately."

"Then the British ambassador?" she said.

"No, he'd probably think we were only inviting him to discuss the Profumo affair."

"But that's business."

"Yes, but a lot of socially prominent people are involved. Internal Revenue might think we were inviting him just to be entertained."

"The Supreme Court, then?"

"It could be awkward. We couldn't say the blessing before the meal."

"What about a few of our friends, then?"

"I told you it had to be people we would write off. None of our friends are deductible."

"But they've entertained us," she protested.

"That's their fault, not ours. How many people do we have so far?"

"None," she said looking down at her list.

"Well, you can't say we didn't try."

My wife became very angry and said sarcastically, "Why don't the two of us have a party and let it go at that?"

"We can't."
"Why not?"
"You're not deductible, either."

THE NUMBERS RACKET

Everyone seems to be in the numbers racket. You can't have a bank account, a charge account, a telephone, or an address without being assigned a number. The purpose of all these numbers, it is carefully explained to the American people, is to help speed up the American way of life. The truth of the matter is that while you do the work for the companies by playing their numbers game, they can lay off thousands of workers and use giant computers instead.

At first the companies were very apologetic about asking you to use your assigned number when making a transaction of any sort. But now they're getting downright mean about it, and if you don't use your number you get hell.

Recently I had the misfortune to spend a few days in Las Vegas, at which time I dropped something in the neighborhood of $150. The casino in question was kind enough to supply me with a blank check. Since I hate to be in debt and also hate to have my arms broken, I wrote out a check for $150 on my bank in New York.

Usually I'm not a sore loser when it comes to gambling debts, but I must say I lost my composure when I received a letter from the bank informing me that, although they had cashed the check as a service, they felt I had done a terrible thing by not putting down the checking number on a blank piece of paper. They felt I was not playing the game, and they advised me in the future to be sure to always write in the number, as it would be difficult to honor numberless checks as they had done in the past.

I wrote back that I, not they, had lost the $150 in Las Vegas, and since I had already gotten bawled out at home, I saw no reason why I should get a lecture from the bank as well. I also pointed out that every time they did anything for me they made a service charge, and since I seemed to be doing their work for them I intended to charge them for it. I told them in the future they would owe 50 cents every time I put down the number on the check.

To spite them further, I informed them I had no intention of putting their postal zip code on the envelope.

I must have frightened them a little, because the next letter was in an apologetic tone.

The Vice-President in Charge of Writing Apologetic Letters informed me he was sorry I was displeased with their system but explained that all checks were processed by machines and there was nobody in the bank who knew how to cash a check by hand. If everyone forgot their checking numbers, he told me, the bank would be forced to hire more people and he was sure I didn't want that.

I might have accepted his explanation except for the fact that at the top of the letter was printed, "In answering this letter please refer to Ref. 2F456-890-B-Z-45."

That did it.

I immediately wrote them:

In reference to your kind letter of 2F456-890-B-Z-45, regarding my checking No. 33-456 000-32, I wish to close my account.

You can send the money to 1346 F Street, N. W., Zip Code 2004, Washington 4, D. C. I am adamant about this, so please do not call me on the phone at area code 202 783-8888 and ask me to reconsider. In answering this letter, please refer to letter reference No. T 345-657-LL W 2.

Sincerely yours,
SWEET SIXTEEN

I haven't heard from the bank yet. I can only hazard a theory as to why. Since the last letter, there is probably nobody at the bank who knows how to read anymore.

FINANCIAL REPORT

The one thing that has emerged from all the hullabaloo about President Johnson's finances is that Mrs. Johnson is probably one of the smartest businesswomen in the United States. Even if you accept the Johnson figures instead of the *Life* magazine figures, it turns out that the Johnsons are millionaires and I only wish my wife had one-twentieth of the business talent of the First Lady.

My wife started investing for me about the same time Mrs.

Johnson started investing for her husband. But unfortunately she chose different investments. The first thing she bought was stock in the Tucker Automobile Co. This cost me $1,000—then the Tucker people decided not to build any cars.

She then decided to get into broadcasting and she invested in a surefire quiz show two days before Charles Van Doren decided to come clean. With the losses from the quiz she decided to buy an Edsel, as she had been given an inside tip that it would have the best resale value of any new car.

It took a few years to get some money back in the bank and when I finally did, my wife put it all in the Suez Canal Co. A week later Nasser nationalized the canal.

Not long after this she heard she could buy a piece of a sugar plantation in Cuba. She was doing great until Castro turned it into a POW camp for the prisoners captured at the Bay of Pigs.

Fortunately I was still on salary at the *Herald Tribune* and I did have a little income. I did until she heard about a fellow named Estes in Texas who was making a fortune for everyone in ammoniated liquid fertilizer tanks. Only by turning government witness did she save us all from going to prison.

With the bail money she decided to take a flyer in salad oil. Her broker told her about a man named Tony D'Angelis who had a fortune in salad oil tied up in New Jersey and who intended to sell the oil to the Russians. She bought half a tank and every day the price skyrocketed. It looked as if I was going to become rich. Then one day some nosy watchman climbed a ladder and decided to look into the tank. You can imagine my wife's surprise when he discovered it was filled with water.

Another woman would have been discouraged by this time, but my wife is made of sterner stuff. Since then she has invested in the Skybolt missile, William Zeckendorf's hotel enterprises, the World Fair's *To Broadway With Love* show which folded, and just the other day she bought a bond issue for fishing rights in the Gulf of Tonkin.

Because of all the publicity about my finances, I have asked the Washington accounting firm of Fagan & Berdansky to release a statement of our holdings.

FINANCIAL POSITION OF
MRS. BUCHWALD

Calvert Food Market..........owes:	$	145.00
Garfinckel's Dept. Store ......owes:		450.00
Heckinger Hardware ....owes:		650.00
Consolidated TV Repair ......owes:		50.00
Doctor's bills................owes:		150.00
Mortgage on house ....owes:		85,000.00

JENNIFER BUCHWALD

Allowance ....$ .25
Piggy bank 1.50

CONNIE BUCHWALD

Notes receivable from Jennifer ....$ .04

JOEL BUCHWALD

Money earned cleaning garage ....$ .75
Bubble gum investment 2.65

FINANCIAL POSITION OF
MR. BUCHWALD

Don't ask.

LOVE IN THE MILLIONS

In May of 1964 20th Century-Fox announced they were suing Elizabeth Taylor and Richard Burton for $50 million in damages in connection with the motion picture *Cleopatra*. The couple were charged with breach of contract and depreciating the commercial value of the movie by their "scandalous" conduct before, and during, the filming of the movie.

When the news was published, Bob Hope said, "Gee, that's going to spoil their honeymoon."

As one of the many combat correspondents who covered the sinking of *Cleopatra* from beginning to end, I was certainly interested in the figure 20th came up with. All of us in Rome knew the Elizabeth Taylor-Burton romance was a hot one, but we never figured it was worth $50 million.

So I went back over my notes to see if the $50 million was justified.

There was one night the couple went out in Rome and Mr. Burton almost socked an Italian photographer. That certainly was worth $5 million to 20th. Then there was another evening when several reporters tried to climb over Miss Taylor's stone wall while Mr. Burton was presumed to be in the house. That was worth $3,500,000 of injury to the reputation of the picture.

On another occasion the couple went for a picnic to the beach with Miss Taylor's children. This cost 20th $4,900,000 in bad publicity.

And then there was that weekend when they went off together and Miss Taylor came back with a swollen eye. I put down $6,100,000 for that incident.

Of course, the big damage was done when they were photographed on a raft together. This was terribly costly to the studio and probably resulted in their losing $7,800,000 in business.

When Eddie Fisher left Rome and Miss Taylor refused to answer his telephone calls, 20th went into a spin. It was a $2,200,000 breach of contract.

Then there were the love scenes at the studio, and while the press agents pretended they were good for the picture, and that people would break down the doors of the theatres to see them on the screen, I knew all along it was costing the Fox people embarrassment to the tune of possibly $5 million.

Then I had several miscellaneous items marked down, such as the couple's being photographed in Roman nightclubs, holding hands on the set and walking down the Via Veneto. Under miscellaneous, I noted $6 million damages.

But this comes to about $40 million, and for the life of me I can't figure why 20th tacked on another $10 million.

I'm sure the studio, which would never take advantage of a publicity stunt, can justify it or they never would have started the suit.

I also owe the executives at 20th Century-Fox an apology. During the filming of the picture, one of the top men said to me, "This picture, in spite of everything, will make $100 million."

I scoffed at the time, but what I didn't know was that Fox planned to get back $50 million of it by suing the stars.

THE UNSOLICITED

One day I received in the mail a magazine I did not subscribe to. I also received a bill from my favorite credit card company for the magazine. When I called up and protested the bill, I was informed that they had sent me a letter the previous month telling me that if they didn't hear from me saying I didn't want the magazine I would automatically be put down for a subscription.

I threw the magazine in the corner with about 100 other items I had been sent without my permission, including books, records, license plates, Indian dolls, birdcages and Christmas cards.

My wife, who is nervous by nature, said, "You've got to send it back."

"Who says so?"

"They do."

"That's how much you know. I didn't ask for their junk and I'm not going to spend the postage to send it back to them."

"I'm afraid."

"They want you to be afraid. They count on it. They're selling by fear," I said.

"I know we're doing something wrong. I'm not sure what it is, but we keep getting bills from all those companies and one day somebody is going to drive up in a police van and take us all away."

In order to calm her I called up a distinguished Washington lawyer, and, after being assured that he wouldn't charge me for the advice, I demanded to know my legal rights in regard to unsolicited gifts.

"What do you do when somebody sends you something you didn't order and demands payment for it or return of the product?"

"Nothing. You don't have to send it back. Nor do you have to pay for it. Of course you can't use it. If you did, that would mean you agree to buy it."

"Can I throw it away?"

"You can after a reasonable amount of time. But it is your duty to keep the product for the person in case he comes back for it. You also have to keep it in good condition."

"Do you mean to say if someone sends me a magazine, I

can't look at it, but I have to keep it in case he comes back for it?"

"Yes, that's the law. Of course you can charge him a storage fee. After all, you are keeping the magazine for him, and it is taking up space. The more magazines you keep for him the higher the storage fee you can charge. Why don't you send them a bill now?"

"What worries me though is, if I don't pay for the subscription, they'll mark me down as a lousy credit risk."

"Good, then you can sue them for slander. If you didn't order something and you refuse to pay for it, they can't very easily say your credit is bad."

The lawyer said that one of the biggest rackets was companies' sending out trinkets under some foundation name and indicating that the proceeds went to charity. "About 30 percent goes for charity, the rest goes into the pockets of the sponsors. The whole business would collapse if people refused to pay for the product and refused to send it back."

"Of course," he said, "I go one step further. When I want to get even with someone who has sent me something I didn't ask for, I take the business reply card or envelope which says, 'No Postage Stamp Necessary If Mailed in the U. S.' and paste it on the largest and heaviest package the Post Office will permit, and send it back to the company. By obligation they have to pay for the postage on the package. I know it's a small thing but I try to strike a blow for freedom whenever I can."

FIRST-CLASS EGYPTIAN

When the Egyptians decided to ship an Israeli citizen air freight from Rome a couple of weeks ago, many people were shocked. But a friend of mine, from Grosse Point, Michigan, saw nothing cruel about the incident at all.

The day after the story broke he called me long distance and said, "Did you see a photo of the trunk they tried to send that fellow in?"

"Yes, it was ghastly, wasn't it?"

"What do you mean, ghastly? Study the picture closely. Doesn't it remind you of anything? Don't you feel you've been there before?"

I studied the picture, but nothing came to mind. "Nope, I can't see it."

"The whole contrivance has been patterned after the three-abreast tourist flights on ——— Airlines. I didn't realize it until I took a flight last week and then it dawned on me where the Egyptians got the idea. Of course the trunk is much more comfortable than the seat on the airline, but that's because the Egyptians take care of their people."

I looked at the picture again. "There is a place to put your head and your feet in the trunk," I said, "which is more than you can say for ——— Airlines."

"Exactly. And there are tiny air holes drilled in the side so the person can breathe."

"You don't get that in tourist class," I had to admit.

"The Egyptians also added another refinement. They administered a drug to the passenger before they sent him off."

"Leave it to the Egyptians to improve air travel."

"You can say that again. Many times just before taking off I've asked the stewardess to shoot something in my arm, but she's always refused."

"Is it against regulations?"

"No, but if they give a shot to one passenger, they have to give it to all the passengers, and they claim they lose money on the route as it is."

"I guess the Egyptians don't care if they make money on *their* flights or not."

"Just as long as they get you there," he said. "But listen, this is what I called you about. I have a friend in the luggage business and I thought we could make up some trunks like the one in the photo for people who can't afford to fly first-class but can't stand to sit three abreast in tourist."

"That's a great idea, but would it sell?"

"We won't sell them; we'll rent them. We could tie up with Hertz or Avis."

"But don't the Egyptians have a patent on the trunk?"

"We'll pay them a royalty and let them use our trunks free of charge in case they want to send anybody else to Cairo."

"It's a very fair offer. What about the drugs?"

"Haven't you ever heard of vending machines?" he asked.

"You've thought of everything," I had to admit.

"From now on there will be three types of travel on a plane—'First-Class,' 'Tourist-Class,' and 'Egyptian-Class.'"

"Manny," I said, "you've done it again."

XI. HOW ARE THINGS IN NONAMURA?

☆☆☆☆☆☆☆☆☆☆☆☆☆☆☆☆☆☆☆☆☆☆☆☆☆

HELP WANTED, TOVARICH

With all their efficiency, the one thing the Soviets forgot to do was take out Khrushchev's hot line to the White House. It probably will be denied, but the other night the hot line rang and Khrushchev was on it.

"Hello, Tovarich, it's Nik," a voice whispered when the President answered the phone.

"Howdy, Mr. Khrushchev! How's everything?"

"Sh, sh, sh, not so loud. They may be listening outside the door. Congratulations on your election."

"Well, thanks very much."

"I imagine you have a lot of jobs open, Tovarich?"

"Well, yes. There are a few appointments I have to make."

"You couldn't use a good Russian expert, could you?"

"I hadn't thought about it. Did you have anybody in mind?"

"Me."

"Gosh, Mr. Khrushchev, that's nice of you to offer, but I don't think I could get you a security clearance. Don't forget you once said you'd bury us, and it's probably in your FBI file."

"I was misquoted, by state controlled Communist press," Mr. K. whispered. "I could make a good Russian expert. I know everything I did wrong in the last twelve years."

"It isn't just the bury-us line that would cause trouble. But remember when you took your shoe off at the United Nations? Well, the security people would probably think you were unstable. They take that kind of thing into consideration."

"Tovarich, I swear on *Das Kapital* the only reason I took

201

my shoe off was because it was too tight. I can say this now. Russian shoes are not very good."

"I'd like to help you, Mr. Khrushchev, but we got too many Russian experts as it is, and I've got an economy drive on. I don't know how I could justify it."

"What about the Department of Agriculture? I'm tops in farming. I could be in charge of collective farms."

"We don't have any collective farms, Mr. Khrushchev."

"I could start some for you," he begged.

"I don't think that would work."

"Is there anything open at Disneyland?"

"I could check for you, but you know that's not a government-owned project. Mr. Disney hires his own people."

"Tovarich, I don't like to beg, but I need a job bad. Could I be a Senator from New York State?"

"We already have one from Massachusetts," the President replied. "Even if there was an opening I'm afraid if you ran they would bring up the carpetbagger issue again."

"There must be something for me to do. Perhaps advertising testimonials. I could be the one who uses greasy kid stuff on his hair."

"I couldn't help you there."

"Maybe baseball Czar?" Nikita said.

"Baseball is America's national pastime. I'm not sure they'd want a Russian to head it up."

"There must be something, Mr. President. After all I did for America these past few years."

"Well, I did hear they were looking for some one to take over the Republican National Committee."

"Wonderful. But wouldn't they object because of my background?"

"It wouldn't bother me."

HOW ARE THINGS IN NONAMURA?

When the country of Nonamura in central Africa started having troubles with tribes in the north, it asked the American ambassador for advice.

The American ambassador said he didn't know much about military affairs, but perhaps the United States, as a gesture of friendship, would send a military adviser to straighten out the matter.

A U. S. Army sergeant was dispatched from Tripoli. In a

few days he wrote his superiors: "I am shocked to find Nonamura soldiers still using poison darts, spears, and World War I rifles. Urge immediate shipment of up-to-date small arms."

The request was approved and the Nonamura army not only received surplus American small arms, but three advisers, led by a captain, to see they were used properly.

The captain and advisers distributed the small arms, but realized that if they were to be effective the Nonamura army would need transportation. The captain cabled: PLEASE SEND U.S. TRUCKS AND WEAPONS CARRIERS WITH TEAM OF TRANS-PORTATION SPECIALISTS AT ONCE AS WAR GOING BADLY IN NORTH.

The transportation specialists, commanded by a major, showed up and after studying the situation the major cabled back: IN ORDER TO MAKE USE OF WEAPONS CARRIERS AND TRUCKS I STRONGLY ADVISE IMMEDIATE DISPATCH OF TANKS, OTHERWISE CANNOT GUARANTEE ARMY VICTORY.

One hundred tanks with 990 tank experts, commanded by a colonel, were shipped in. Unfortunately, while the colonel was setting up the tank school, the rebel tribesmen overran a government position and stole most of the weapons supplied by the U. S.

(The rest were sold at bargain prices to the rebels by a corrupt minister of defense.)

The colonel flew back to Washington to make a report. He advised the Pentagon to replenish the stolen weapons and, while they were at it, to include some flamethrowers, rockets, antiaircraft guns, and long-range artillery.

The Pentagon took the colonel's advice and the equipment was sent with a division of advisers from Fort Benning, Georgia, commanded by a major general.

He no more than got settled when he shot off a wire to the Joint Chiefs of Staff: IMPOSSIBLE MAKE ANY HEADWAY IN NONAMURA WITHOUT AIR SUPPORT. STRONGLY ADVISE YOU SEND TWO SQUADRONS OF F-105 FIGHTER AIRCRAFT TRAINING PERSONNEL. CANNOT BE RESPONSIBLE FOR WHAT HAPPENS WITHOUT AIR COVER.

The Joint Chiefs sent two squadrons of jet aircraft and an entire training wing supplied by the Navy and headed up by a vice-admiral.

Unfortunately at that moment the Nonamura government was overthrown and replaced by a military junta. The admiral cabled Washington: CORRUPT CIVILIAN GOVERNMENT REPLACED BY SERIOUS NONAMURA GENERALS. STRONGLY URGE YOU RECOGNIZE AT ONCE AND GIVE THEM $50 MILLION LOAN.

A month later a U. S. Air Force four-star general, who had replaced the admiral, wired the State Department: CORRUPT MILITARY JUNTA REPLACED BY PRO-WEST NONAMURA COLONELS. WE MUST BACK THEM IF WE HOPE TO DEFEAT REBELS.

By this time Congress and the press were getting interested. We had 200,000 military advisers in Nonamura. The President did the only thing he could do under the circumstances. He sent his Secretary of Defense to give him a firsthand report. The Secretary cabled the President: WAR GOING WELL BUT NONAMURA NEEDS MORE MILITARY AID AND LACKS ONLY $124 MILLION.

This was immediately voted by Congress.

In spite of everything things still aren't going too well in Nonamura. Just the other day the President received a request from the Joint Chiefs of Staff. All it said was: WOULD YOU HAVE ANY OBJECTION IF WE LENT NONAMURA 10 OBSOLETE ATOMIC BOMBS?

FRUSTRATION IN RED CHINA

Not so long ago, 700,000 angry and frustrated Chinese gathered in Peking's Tien An Man Square to demonstrate against American intervention in the Congo. The tragedy was that there was no American embassy to demonstrate against. This points up as well as anything why the recognition of Red China should be reconsidered.

Had we had an American embassy in Peking and a USIA library, the Chinese would have probably broken every window in the building and burned up every book, as the Indonesians did in Jakarta. This would have given the United States an opportunity to present a strong protest to the Chinese and demand immediate payment for the damage to our embassy.

The fact that we have no relations with Red China makes it impossible to protest to them about wrecking our embassy and prevents us from collecting money for the damage to USIA books.

Furthermore, the fact that the Chinese had no American embassy to vent their anger against has caused them to hate us more than even our actions in the Congo. It's pretty tough to parade through the streets of Peking for hours on end without any place to march on.

In Moscow, during the same period, the Soviets marched on the American embassy and did as much damage as the Soviet police would let them. The Russians went away happy, with a warm spot in their hearts for Americans, and ever since the demonstrations relations between the United States and Russia have improved.

An observer in Cairo reports that the Egyptians have never felt better than they have since they burned up the USIA library and wrecked the U. S. Marine barracks.

But Peking is still a mass of seething students and workers whose anger is bottled up inside them.

Unless America does something to release this anger, we could be confronted with a serious international problem which eventually may become insoluble.

Although American policy is still against the recognition of Red China, there are other solutions which could be worked out.

One might be to build an American embassy in Peking without recognizing the Communist government. The building would be designed to withstand the assaults of the largest type of Red Chinese demonstration, but would also have enough windows so the demonstrators could let off steam.

We wouldn't have to staff the embassy with anyone except repairmen and glaziers who could handle the damage.

After two or three demonstrations against the U. S. embassy, the Chinese would be so happy they might start demonstrating against the Peking government, demanding a rapprochement with the United States.

In return for this, the United States would also benefit. If Peking built an embassy in Washington, it would give our students a chance to demonstrate against the Red Chinese over their aid to North Vietnam.

Before long the two countries would be trying to burn down each other's embassies and you would have normal diplomatic relations between two of the great powers in the world. It's something for Dean Rusk to think about.

WHAT IS DE GAULLE UP TO?

Just because I lived in France for fourteen years, people are constantly coming up to me and saying, "What is General de Gaulle up to?"

If I reply that I have no idea what General de Gaulle is up to, they think I'm holding out on them. So I've decided to violate a friendship of years and reveal what General de Gaulle really has on his mind.

I first met General de Gaulle in 1961 at the Élysée Palace at a reception for 2,000 members of the diplomatic corps and press. I was standing in line as he walked by, and he stopped in front of me and asked in French, "Do you know all the people in this room?"

"Oui, mon général," I replied.

He nodded and walked on.

And so I can honestly say I have not only seen General de Gaulle, but I've spoken to him.

From this lengthy encounter I can give an honest assessment of what General de Gaulle is up to. In the give and take of a frank conversation such as I reported above, the General said exactly what was on his mind, and I in turn told him exactly what I thought. I think he respected me for it.

The first thing you must realize if you want to understand General de Gaulle is that he is very tall, and can usually see over everybody's head. Most people have to look up to him and he in turn must look down on everybody. When I spoke to him my nose came up to the third button of his tunic, which put me at somewhat of a disadvantage. I have always believed you can never trust a man who doesn't look you straight in the eye.

In this case, I stared straight into his tunic button, and the tunic button stared straight back.

General de Gaulle, when he is standing still, has a military bearing which should tell a lot about him. When he speaks, his voice comes from deep inside of him, which makes his tunic button hop up and down. Since you are staring at it, you keep nodding your head up and down to follow his conversation, and therefore he thinks you are agreeing with him. Many diplomats have been caught this way and have regretted the consequences later.

In our conversation I gathered that it is not what General de

Gaulle said, but what he didn't say, which is important. He didn't say, for example, that he planned to keep Great Britain out of the Common Market, or that he would continue to test his bomb, or that he would recognize Red China, or that he would visit South America.

And yet I had the feeling talking to him that he intended to do all those things. The inflection in his voice when he said, "Do you know all the people in this room?" left no doubt in my mind that he intended to continue a course of unilateral action even at the cost of dividing the West.

I also feel that my response of "Oui, mon général" had some effect on his future plans. After all, I happened to be an American journalist and had I said, "Non, mon général," he might have changed his ideas.

Many people have spoken to General de Gaulle since then, but I don't think anyone has ever gotten as close to him as I did.

And so when people now ask me, "What is General de Gaulle up to?" I reply, "I don't know what he is up to, but I'm up to the third tunic button on his chest."

HEAD OF THE CLASS

Probably the toughest thing to be in this world is a Soviet student. No matter how well you learn your lessons, it doesn't necessarily mean you're right.

For example, last October at People's School 113 in Moscow, a teacher was talking to his eighth-grade class.

"Boys and girls, today the brave Soviet cosmonauts, Komarov, Yegorov, and Feoktistov, have returned from their glorious flight into space. The first question is: Who is the man who is responsible for this unbelievable feat?"

The children shout, "Comrade Khrushchev!"

"Why is Comrade Khrushchev responsible, little Vladimir?"

"Because, Comrade Teacher, he is our glorious leader, and he has sent our spaceships into the heavens to show the decadent Western capitalist nations the Soviets are first in science."

"Very good, Vladimir. Now, little Katrina, what else has our beloved Comrade Khrushchev done?"

"He has kept the peace in the world, has spread the message

of Communism throughout the globe, and has brought prosperity to the peoples of all the Soviets."

"What else, Ivan?"

"He has made the corn grow high, the wheat grow strong, and the flowers bloom."

"And what about steel production?"

"That's good, too."

"Little Boris, who is the greatest leader against the reactionary adventurist and chauvinist line of the Chinese government?"

"I don't know."

"Stupid lout, Boris. What do you mean, you don't know?"

"I'm not sure."

"Stay after class, Boris, and we will see if we can refresh your memory."

As he is talking, the principal comes in and whispers something into the teacher's ear. The teacher goes white. He nods and writes down some things on a pad.

Then he addresses the class again. "Now, once more. Who is the man who is responsible for our great victory over space?"

"Comrade Khrushchev," the class shouts.

"Idiots! How many times do I have to tell you? It is our glorious leader, Leonid Brezhnev, the enemy of the cult of personality and brother of the working classes."

He looks at little Vladimir.

"Now tell me, little Vladimir, what has Comrade Khrushchev done?"

"He has sent our spaceships into the heavens—"

"Stop! Comrade Khrushchev is a reactionary phrasemonger, a harebrained, inept, bragging fool, and an enemy of the people."

Katrina raises her hand. "But did he not keep the peace in the world?"

"Daughter of an imperialist! If I've told you once, I've told you a hundred times, Aleksei Nikolaevich Kosygin is a man of peace. Khrushchev is a drunkard, and a criminal with paranoid tendencies."

"But it says in the book—"

"Never mind the book! They are all going to be confiscated. I am ashamed of all of you for not learning your lessons. The only one who has done his homework is little Boris. Little Boris will someday be a great Communist leader."

THE SEARCH THAT FAILED

The search for qualified women in government goes on and on and on. President Johnson wanted 50 women for high government positions, but so far he hasn't been doing too well. What are the reasons behind this failure?

I'm quite sure there are 50 qualified women in the United States for government service. I know of one who happens to be married to me and she's constantly seeking government work. Just the other day she said, "I'll do anything to get out of this house."

"But what job could you do?" I asked her.

"I'd like a job that would take me to Paris twice a year, permit me to fly to Hong Kong and Tokyo, and provide me with a cook and a chauffeur at government expense."

"You mean you want to be the Secretary of State?"

"I guess so, if that's what they call it."

"What makes you think you would be able to handle foreign affairs?"

"I don't think it's difficult."

"Well, how would you solve the Cuban crisis?"

"I'd give them buses. That's what they want, isn't it?"

"You can't give them buses. We have no relations with them."

"That's why I'd give them buses. It seems to me that every time we break off relations with a country France or Great Britain immediately offers to sell them buses. Then we get mad at our friends and they get mad at us and we start fighting among ourselves. If we gave the Cubans the buses, then our allies wouldn't be mad at us."

"That shows how little you know about foreign affairs," I said. "Britain and France aren't mad at us because we won't sell Cuba any buses. They're grateful. If it wasn't for us, they wouldn't have anybody to buy their buses. Every time we break off relations with a country, it opens up a new bus market for them."

"Then why are they mad at us?"

"Because we won't sell them any ammunition for their pistols. A year ago we tried to give Britain and France atomic bombs. But now, because they're trading with Cuba, we won't give them bullets for their guns. That's why they're mad."

"Why do France and Britain need bullets?" she wanted to know.

"Because they have to stop the troubles in Gabon and Cyprus. They need our small arms to do it."

"I don't understand," she said.

"It's quite simple. Congress is furious at Britain and France for trading with Castro. In order to placate Congress, the State Department has to show it's taking a hard line, so we have cut off military aid to our two strongest allies. Unfortunately, the military aid consists of small arms. France and Britain say that if we sell wheat to Russia they should be able to sell buses to Castro.

"But we say they wouldn't talk that way if Castro cut off their water.

"We want France to help us against Cuba, but we don't want her interfering in Vietnam, and Britain wants us to help her in Cyprus, but they don't want us interfering in her trade with Castro. Now do you understand?"

She was silent for a moment, and then she said, "No wonder they can't get any women to work in the government."

A BULL IN A CHINA SHOP

This business of recognizing Red China is getting very complicated. Everything was going along fine until General de Gaulle decided to recognize her. Then everything went wrong.

Red China told de Gaulle that if he recognized her he couldn't recognize Nationalist China. But General de Gaulle insists he must recognize two Chinas as a condition for recognizing Red China. At the same time, de Gaulle seems to be doing his utmost to get Chiang's China to break off diplomatic relations with France so he won't be bothered with two Chinese ambassadors.

The United States very wisely recognized only one China, or Nationalist China, which isn't China at all but Taiwan. The reasoning behind this is quite simple. Red China is giving us so much trouble in Southeast Asia that it's better to pretend she doesn't exist.

If we recognized Red China, which consists of 800 million people, then we would be letting down Nationalist China, which has a population of 11,613,000. We have a big stake in Nationalist China, but none whatsoever in Red China except getting in a war with them over Indochina, which is now called Vietnam.

It must be pointed out that recognition of a country doesn't guarantee you're going to have better relations with them. The Soviet Union was the first country to recognize Red China and they seem to be worse off than we are. And the minute de Gaulle announced that he was going to recognize Red China, the Chinese started fighting with him over Nationalist China.

Then what are the advantages of recognizing Red China? The greatest one is that if we recognize her we can then call her names. It's very difficult to call anyone names whose existence is in doubt. And, if we recognize Communist China, we would be able to prove in the United Nations that she was an aggressor and should be thrown out for violating the UN charter. This would be a big propaganda coup for us, and might possibly make the Red Chinese get in line.

But there are disadvantages to recognizing her. Besides alienating Chiang Kai-shek, which no American would think of doing, you also run the tremendous risk that Red China might do a complete about-face and, in exchange for a coexistence policy, demand foreign aid from us.

The United States just can't afford to take care of 800 million starving Chinese at this time, and our whole economy would be ruined if we tried. The big fear then is not that the Red Chinese would remain at odds with us, but that they would try to adjust their differences, which would force us to help them out.

What is the solution? Quite simple. There should be a third China set up somewhere, which would have nothing to do with the other two Chinas. This would be a Neutralist China, neither Communist nor Nationalist. It could be located in Liechtenstein or in Switzerland. This China would be palatable to everyone and recognition of it would not be contingent on the recognition of the other two Chinas.

Thus we would avoid the situation now facing France, and inevitably facing the United States. For when the day comes that we can't prevent the United Nations from recognizing Red China, we're going to be in a lot of trouble with Nationalist China. If we had a third China to recognize, it would mean we could line up two Chinas against their one.

The more Chinas there are in the world the happier everybody should be.

HOW TO ORGANIZE A COUP

"Gentlemen, the class will come to order. Today we will discuss the organizing of military coups. As you know, when you return to your own countries at the end of this course, you will be in charge of large units of your national army. You will probably be involved with at least one coup and there are certain things you must be aware of. First of all, what kind of a coup do you want?"

A colonel raises his hand. "A bloodless coup?"

"Very good, Colonel Phununumu. A bloodless coup is always the best kind. World opinion will always accept a bloodless coup, whereas if you have to resort to fighting it will look messy in the newspapers and you will give all military coups a bad name.

"In order to organize a bloodless coup, you have to have a junta. This junta should be composed of other officers, preferably below the rank of general. When your coup is successful, you can promote yourselves. Actually, one of the main reasons for a coup is to speed up the promotion process in the military services. What is it, Major Gonzales?"

"Señor, eef we 'ave a junta, who decides who eez the chief?"

"You cut cards for it. That's usually the way it's done."

A naval captain raises his hand. "In most bloodless coups the army seems to get all the jobs and the navy is rarely consulted. Is there anything we can do to play a bigger role?"

"It all depends where the capital of your country is. If the capital is a seaport, you can bring in your destroyers and cruisers and threaten to shell the city if you're not made part of the junta. By the same token, you men in the air force can indicate that you'll bomb the capital if you're not given a role. Ideally, military coups should be split amongst all the armed services.

"Now the most important thing in a coup is to get command of troops. A tank corps command is ideal or a paratrooper command is quite helpful. Stay off the general staff if you possibly can. You may get arrested by mistake.

"Once you have command of troops, you must think of some excuse to bring them into the capital of the country. Perhaps you can bring them in for an armed forces loyalty day parade or a USO show. Fix your arrival for early in the morning when everyone is sleeping. The first thing you do is to surround the Presidential palace and the radio station. You announce over the radio that you have taken over in the name of free and democratic government and you charge the incumbents with stealing the treasury, setting up a dictatorship, and dealing with subversive foreign powers.

"If all goes well, you should be in the palace for breakfast. Put the President and his Cabinet under house arrest and organize a popular demonstration in the streets. Let the people burn down a department store or a foreign embassy to make them feel they really have freedom. After that, move in your troops and put in a seven o'clock curfew on the town.

"Then hold a press conference and announce that none of the foreign policies of your country will change and you will be happy to accept aid from any country which offers it without strings. You will be surprised how anxious foreign diplomats are to get in good with a new junta. You had a question, Colonel Choo?"

"Only one. How do we open a Swiss bank account?"

WHY RUSSIANS DEFECT

There has been a lot of talk in the newspapers lately about Russian defectors. I've always wondered why Russians defect and the other day I was fortunate to interview one who gave me some interesting details on his defection.

I shared a table with him at Bassin's Cafeteria and introduced myself. He said:

"I am Nicolai Sergevitch, Russian defector."

"I'm very pleased to meet you, sir. I haven't met many Russian defectors."

"Is nice meeting you," he replied. "I don't meet many people who put chutney on knockwurst."

"May I ask you a personal question? Why did you defect?"

"It is a simple story," he said. "I am big shot in Soviet government. I have my own car, my own bureau, my own dacha. I am up-and-coming Communist commissar. No one has better future than me."

"I don't understand. You didn't hate Russia, then?"

"Hate? I loved Russia. It is my motherland. Even now I miss it."

"Then why did you defect?"

"One day I am called in by my superior and he says, 'Nicolai, we are sending you to United States of America on top-secret mission. We trust you as loyal Soviet Communist, but just to make certain that you come back we are going to keep your wife behind. If anything goes wrong you know what will happen to her.'

"I say, 'Don't worry, Comrade Guzenko. I am loyal to the motherland. You can count on me.' So I go home and tell my wife I am going on top-secret mission and she is getting sick and tired of it, and she is fed up with running a hotel, and I should do some other type work because a wife she is not, and I am a lousy husband because I never give her enough money, and on and on and on. Then her mother, who is living with us, says her daughter should have never married below her class, and maybe because I probably have a girl friend somewhere, and on and on and on.

"So off I go to United States of America. Every day I get letters from wife telling me plumbing is no good, neighbors is making too much noise, she can't buy any curtains, window in cellar is broken, her mother is out of job, and everything is lousy. She says wait until I get home, because she is really going to tell me a thing or two and she is not going to take my going away lying down.

"After two weeks of letters I say to myself, 'America is not such a bad country after all. Maybe I will become a defector.' "

"But," I said, "what about your wife? Didn't they tell you if you refused to come back they would do something to her?"

"Exactly, comrade," he smiled. "You are now eating with a man who committed a perfect crime."

"GIVE US THIS DAY"

I have this Russian friend and every once in a while we get into long arguments over the merits of the Russian vs. the American system.

"Well, Vladimir," I said to him one day back in October of 1963, "it looks as if your system has failed."

"How is that?"

"You have to buy wheat from us because your agricultural production has been a disaster."

"Yes, and you have to sell us the wheat because if you don't you won't be able to balance your gold payments."

"We don't have to sell you wheat. We're doing it out of the goodness of our heart."

"And $300 million dollars you will receive for it."

"Vladimir, you know the Communist system is a flop. If we didn't send you wheat, your people would be up in arms."

"And if you didn't get rid of your surplus wheat, your people would be up in arms. By buying your wheat we are saving the capitalist system."

"Don't talk foolish. We are the richest country in the world. That is why we have surpluses."

"Yes, but what can you do with the surpluses? We are the only ones who will buy your wheat. I personally am against the deal because, if we want the capitalist system to fail, we should not support it by trading with you."

"And I am against the deal because, if the Communist system ever collapses, it will be because you cannot produce enough crops to feed your people."

"It is not our system, but the weather that has failed. We are not responsible for acts of God."

"Aha! So you admit there is a God."

"Only when it comes to crop failures."

"Vladimir, have you ever heard the verse, 'Give us this day our daily bread and forgive us our trespasses as we forgive those who trespass against us'?"

"It's written in the wheat deal?"

"No, it's from the Bible. Well, anyway, it doesn't apply in your case. We're willing to give you bread, but we can't forgive you for trespassing. The only thing we ask of you is that you tell the Russian people they are eating American wheat."

"We will if you tell the American people Russia is solving your surplus problems."

"We're selling you wheat at a great risk, Vladimir, and I think you should be grateful. For one thing, we used to sell the wheat to West Germany and they made flour from it and then sold it to you. They are very angry that we're selling the wheat direct."

"Why don't you be honest and admit you don't care what the Germans think since they won't buy your chickens anyway? You know, if we like your wheat, we might buy other things from you. Since you're practically out of the Common Market you're going to need us in the future. We could be good customers."

"We do not wish to trade with someone who has a different system than ours."

"You're crazy. For years you have been trading with countries that have the same system. As each country develops its own industry, it is making the same product as your country. Before you know it you are in competition with all your friends. So the only markets left open to you are those of your enemies. Whether you like it or not, you have to trade with us for the good of your own economy."

"But, Vladimir, there is one flaw in your argument. Where will you get the money to pay us for our stuff?"

"What's the matter? You've never heard of the Marshall Plan?"

RUSSIAN COMMISSAR DEFECTS

A fellow came in the office one day looking for a job.

"Comrade Igor Ilitchev," he said. "I'm a Russian defector."

"Glad to meet you, Comrade," I said. "Couldn't stand the Communist system, eh?"

"No," he replied, "I liked Communist system. I believed in Soviet Union 100 percent."

"Then why did you defect?"

"I didn't exactly defect. They threw me out."

"Why was that, Comrade?"

"I was too anti-American."

"I don't understand," I said.

So he tearfully told me his story. "I was in charge of writing all anti-American speeches in Soviet Union. Big job, no? I was the one who wrote 'imperialist warmongers,' 'capitalist dogs,' 'colonialist pigs,' and 'bloodsucking leeches of the almighty dollar.' It was I who invented phrase, 'We will bury you!' Whenever someone had to speak at Communist Congress meeting, United Nations, or summit conference against Americans, they would say, 'Get Ilitchev, Commissar of Invective.' "

"You did have an important job," I said.

"And what is more, I liked my work," he said. "I thought of words in English that even Americans had never heard of. I was secure and I was sure I had a lifetime job."

"I should hope so," I said.

"Hah, that's how much you know about Soviet system!

"A month ago I am called in by Comrade Gromyko. 'Comrade,' he says, 'I make speech at United Nations in September. Give me two hours of extemporaneous talk.'

"I go to my typewriter and I let out all stops. I prove Americans using germ warfare in Vietnam, that they are kidnapping doctors in Cuba, bribing labor leaders in Italy, planning atomic war in Kashmir, enslaving natives in the Katanga, sending submarines to Israel, violating truces in Korea. It was fine speech and it moved my secretary so much, when she typed it, that she went to U. S. Embassy in Moscow and started throwing ink bottles against the wall.

"I give to Gromyko and he says, 'Comrade, this is too anti-American. I must have conciliatory speech. Something to ease the Cold War. This makes me sound like Chinese deviationist.'

"I get angry and say, 'Comrade Gromyko, I have been writing speeches about America for years. I know what the public wants.'

"He says, 'Comrade, we may disagree with the Americans on many things, but we must never call them names. I'm afraid we're going to have to bring in some coexistence writers from Siberia.'

"Well, I know when I'm not wanted, so I defect. It's either that or going to Siberia until Cold War starts up again."

"That's a very interesting and sad story, but I don't know how I could help you find a job," I said.

"I thought perhaps with American elections coming up," he said, "someone could use good invective writer. I brought out all my anti-Johnson speeches with me. Who would know they were written by a Russian?"

JUMP IN THE LAKE

Recently we had a week known as "Tell the United States to Jump in the Lake Week." Between General Khanh in Vietnam, the African nations in the UN and our good and dear friend Nasser in the United Arab Republic, everyone seemed to be giving us the business and there wasn't much we could do about it.

Nobody seems to be impressed with the power and influence of the United States these days.

Just the other day the Prime Minister of the newly formed country of Disdainia paid a visit to the American Embassy to ask the American ambassador for aid.

"Mr. Ambassador," he said, "our country is in dire straits. Our agricultural crops have failed, our textile industry is bankrupt and our five-year housing plan has been abandoned. We need American help immediately."

"Then why are your people breaking all the windows in my embassy?" the ambassador asked.

"I must warn you, Mr. Ambassador, we will not accept any aid that has strings attached. Our country has its pride."

"I'm not asking for strings," the ambassador replied. "I'm asking you to stop breaking my windows."

"My government will not permit your government to tell us how to run our internal affairs."

"Mr. Prime Minister, why did you burn down the USIA library?"

"I will not sit here and listen to these colonialist attacks against my country. We are a free nation and we can burn down any library we feel like."

The American ambassador ducks as a rock comes flying through the window. "Another thing, Mr. Prime Minister. My country would like to know why your country shot down three unarmed American airplanes?"

"And what about the way you treat Negroes in the South?" the Prime Minister said.

The American ambassador clutched his desk as a bomb went off in the Embassy basement. "It's going to be hard for me to justify American aid in your country when you keep doing things that offend our country."

"Be more specific, Mr. Ambassador."

"Well, for example, I thought making me eat an American flag at your Independence Day celebration was a bit much."

"We made the Russian ambassador eat a flag also and he didn't complain."

"That's because you tipped him off and he had one made of rice paper."

"I didn't come here to discuss trivial matters. I came to ask for agricultural items, a couple of hydroelectric dams and three squadrons of jet bombers. I feel that's the least you can do for a new nation that is struggling to join the family of peace-loving nations."

"What about those American missionaries you're holding as hostages?"

"What about the 800 students you arrested at the University of California?"